HEROINES AND HYSTERICS

Heroines and Hysterics

Mary R. Lefkowitz

St Martin's Press New York

For Cousin Nan

γυναῖκές ἐσμεν, φιλόφρον ἀλλήλαις γένος
σῴζειν τε κοινὰ πράγματ' ἀσφαλέσταται.

© 1981 by Mary R. Lefkowitz

ISBN 0 312 37160 8

Library of Congress Cataloging in Publication Data

Lefkowitz, Mary R., 1935 –
Heroines and hysterics.

Includes bibliographical references and index.
1. Classical literature – History and criticism.
2. Women in literature.
3. Feminism.
I. Title.
PA3016.W7L4 1981 880'.09'352042 81-9387

ISBN 0-312-37160-8 AACR2

Contents

Preface

Until Sarah Pomeroy's *Goddesses, Whores, Wives and Slaves* was published in 1975 little had appeared in print that called attention to the realities of women's life in the ancient world. The women one had read about were famous by male standards of achievement or notoriety, the few great women writers, the companions or mothers of famous men. The civil rights movement of the 1960s had encouraged scholars (mostly women) to draw attention to discrimination against women in Greece and Rome. Certain documents were singled out for their hostility – Hesiod's *Works and Days*, Semonides' poem on women, Juvenal's Sixth Satire – and attention was drawn to destructive heroines like Clytemnestra or Medea. But Sarah Pomeroy was the first to assemble and discuss all forms of evidence together. Her work suggests that any document or genre offers only a partial view of the whole, and that to understand women's life in the ancient world a great variety of sources must be read and approaches for commenting on them defined.

I had myself begun in the early 1970s to discuss issues that I felt had been ignored in traditional criticism. Why did myths about women follow certain patterns only? Why was Sappho's poetry criticised for the nature of its content and its style? When I eagerly accepted an invitation in 1975 to compile a book of sources about ancient women, I did not imagine how difficult the task would be.

No great ancient writer devoted himself or herself to the task of writing a woman's biography, or wanted to describe the workings of an actual household or shop (or brothel) over a period of time; all types of documents could be considered relevant, fragments of poetry, speeches from comedy, as well as inscriptions and papyrus contracts. Trying to put the different texts into context for non-professional readers led me to realise that there was a major need to demonstrate how to present the sources so that their meaning would not be distorted or their purpose misunderstood. Also, since so much essential information had been lost, there seemed reason to suggest ways of combining different sources, keeping in mind the limitations imposed by their nature and their context.

These were the aims that I had in mind when I began to write the other chapters that make up this book. I have tried to ask myself how contemporary experience or theories can affect our understanding of the past; conversely, I have tried to discover how ancient views of women's life and mind continue to influence our present thinking. I have tried to address myself to questions raised over and over again by feminist criticism. What were women in drama supposed to represent to their audiences? How close does literature come to other perceptions of the realities of women's life? If my answers are not comprehensive, it is due to the nature of the evidence as well as the limits of my knowledge. For example, we can only *assume* that when Medea says she would rather fight in three battles than bear one child, it is because she fears in both experiences equal pain and danger. Greek gravestones offer only scattered testimony of women's death in childbirth, and information about the mother's age only if she was very young. Other societies with comparably limited medical expertise may serve as analogues, but too imprecisely to permit us to be certain whether women in general shared Medea's views.

Studying women's choruses and choral songs has led me to reflect how little recognition was accorded to women's own accomplishments. Women are praised and praise each other for their beauty, that is, how they appear to others. A girl might win a vase for skill in carding wool, but there were no prizes for artistic achievement in weaving. When the Spartan princess Cynisca won at the Olympic games, a male professional drove her chariot. No woman in Greek literature succeeds without assistance; either she has a male protector or a group of female friends. In real life as well, a woman could not conduct a transaction without the consent of a male guardian. She grew up as a member of a *hēlikia*, or age-group, who celebrated her wedding and mourned her death along with members of her family. Iphigenia counts on the women in the chorus to conspire in her rescue of Orestes: 'We are women; as a race, we think kindly of each other; we can count on each other to protect our common aims.' When a woman is singled out from the group, a change occurs in her status: she is about to be married or carried off, or heading for some other danger: we know Antigone is in trouble when her sister Ismene refuses to go with her.

The superficial similarities to our own world are only too apparent; they have helped me to understand, though not always applaud, the conditions of ancient women's life. Had I lived at another time or in another country, I doubt that I should have been encouraged to try to describe the crucial differences between male and female existence. Women's colleges have been said to be the last places where such issues would be discussed; yet I believe that it is because I have spent so much of my life with other women that I have been able to realise that my responses to what I have read are not unique.

It might be objected that I have concentrated more on the limitations than on the potentialities of women's lives. Again the negative emphasis derives from the kinds of materials I have worked with. Medical treatises describe disease, not health; drama and legal cases deal with problems; epitaphs and martyrologies record deaths. Myth concerns forces beyond human control, not the comfortable reassurance of a successful routine or relationship. But there is no question that analogous documents for the lives of men present a more positive picture: they do not have so wide a repertory of diseases of the reproductive tract; they had the ability to take decisions and to act without assistance; they could leave behind them monuments that later generations would admire and remember.

We are justified in studying Classical antiquity because of the clarity with which Greek and Roman writers describe their world, and for their continuing desire to define and to come to terms with fundamental issues. The Greeks were the first people openly to discuss the difficulties of women's life. If they failed to offer anything other than theoretical solutions, they were only being realistic. The essays at the end of this book discuss ancient and modern notions of how women might become independent. I wonder whether the audience who listened to the story of Io's wandering in the *Prometheus Bound* would think contemporary society offered women any significant psychological advantage.

Acknowledgments for permission to reprint are due as follows. Chapter 3: *New England Classical News Letter*, vol.6, no 3 (1979). Chapter 5: D. G. McGuigan (ed.), *A Sampler of Women's Studies*, 1973. Chapter 6: *The Spectator*, 24 November 1979. Chapter 7: *Classical World* 73.1 (1979). Chapter 8: *Journal of the American Academy of Religion* 44/3 (1976). Chapter 9: *Greek, Roman and Byzantine Studies*, vol.14, no 2 (1973). Chapter 10: *Classical World*, November 1973. Chapter 11: *Signs,* vol.2, no 3 (1977). Chapter 12: *Carleton Miscellany,* vol.18, no 2 (1980). Chapter 13: *American Journal of Philology* 98 (1977). Chapter 14: *Chronicle of Higher Education*, 6 August 1979. Chapter 15: *Classical Journal*, vol.68, no 1 (1972). Chapters 1, 2, 4 and 16 are hitherto unpublished.

1981   M.R.L.

1

Women's Heroism

When considered from a feminist perspective, the plots of Greek mythology present a frightening view of female experience. A woman can keep her identity only by remaining a virgin, like the goddesses Athena and Artemis, or by destroying or abandoning her male partner, like Aphrodite, or Clytemnestra, or Medea. Marriage is death, either literally, or figuratively, as for Semele or Io, whose stories end with the birth of their sons. One could regard Penelope as yet another example of a woman who is important only while her husband is absent, since the moment he returns, she disappears from view.[1]

But when one reflects on what women say and do within the confines of the traditional plots, positive values emerge. The poets, particularly Homer and Euripides, seem to have used female experience as a foil to the essentially destructive heroism their works were primarily intended to celebrate. Penelope herself may be the best example. Odysseus identifies himself to Alcinous as 'known to men for all his deceptions' (doloi, Od.9.19-20). But the audience of the Odyssey hears first about Penelope, who had deceived the suitors for four years with her deception (dolos) about Laertes' shroud (Od.2.93), and it is Penelope who manages to deceive even Odysseus by telling Eurycleia to move his bed (Od.23.176ff.). When she finally acknowledges that he is Odysseus, Homer compares them to survivors of a shipwreck: 'only a few have escaped the grey sea and swum ashore; much salt clings to their skin; gladly they step on to land, after escaping from evil'(Od.23.236-8). The description recalls Odysseus' own struggle to swim ashore on Phaeacia (Od.5.388).

Odysseus cannot complete his return until, like Penelope, he relies on intelligence and patience more than on traditional masculine virtues of brute force and anger. At the beginning of his voyage back, he acts like an Achilles, sacking the city of the Cicones; but soon heroic methods prove less successful: to escape from the Cyclops he is forced to rely on the kind of calculated guile that enabled Penelope to fend off the suitors. It is an Odysseus who has

[1]For an extreme point of view, see below, ch.5.

learned to wait, to restrain himself, to depend on the help of others, like Ino/Leucothea, the Phaeacians and Athena, who finally manages to get home. And it is significant that he wins his greatest successes, both in Phaeacia and in Ithaca, in disguise, without his heroic identity, his titles, patronymics, and reference to the victory he won at Troy. The false stories he tells about his background help to emphasise the futility of the heroic existence, a life spent fighting, away from home and family.

When Demodocus sings about the Trojan horse, Odysseus weeps like a woman who has lost her husband who had been fighting to defend his country (*Od*.8.521ff.). When he first speaks to Penelope in Book 19 he compares her renown to a king's whose country is strong and prosperous. Penelope has won her renown (*kleos*) not simply by remaining faithful to her husband, but because of her resistance to the suitors, and her deceiving them for four years by weaving and unweaving Laertes' shroud (*Od*.19.107ff.). Frequent references to Helen and Clytemnestra remind us of the damage she might have caused her country or her husband had she done otherwise. Penelope provides an example of how *kleos* can be achieved not by killing others, or by demanding honour, like Achilles in the *Iliad*.

But the *Iliad* also offers influential examples of women's heroism. Aristotle of course says that the dramatic mimesis in the *Iliad* and the *Odyssey* outlined the form (*schemata*) of tragedy (*Poetics* 1448b-1449a); Homer's description of Hector's self-delusion and final recognition anticipates what the tragic poets will concentrate on.[2] Achilles, for all his intelligence, does not realise the full consequences of his anger, which will result in Patroclus' as well as in his own death. Like other Homeric heroes, he is more concerned with his honour than with the welfare of his close friends and relatives. Hector returns to battle in *Iliad* 6 and 22 because he is ashamed of what the Trojan men and women will say of him (*Il*.6.442-3); he cannot stay safe behind the walls as Andromache sensibly suggests. Sophocles' *Ajax* kills himself rather than accept the limitations of his understanding and of his power.

In the man's world of war which is the subject of the *Iliad* women appear only at intervals. They are valuable property: the Greeks come to restore a woman who was stolen from her husband; Achilles becomes angry and refuses to fight because Agamemnon takes his Briseis away. Women are dependent upon men for their status in life and the mode of their existence; they are unable to take action on

[2]Chicago 1975, 125-6. On the delusion inflicted on men by the gods in Homer, see H. Lloyd-Jones, *The Justice of Zeus* (Berkeley 1971) 24: 'The human agent knows what is right, but the god overbears his will'; in Soph., *Ant.* also, Zeus leads human reason toward *atē* (p.112).

their own. But their helplessness gives them another kind of independence: as outsiders, they can comment as observers on what is happening around them, since they are on the walls of Troy or in the Greek camp and not on the battlefield. Andromache, for instance, understands more completely than Hector what the outcome of the war will be.[3] He says in *Iliad* 6 that he knows there will come a day when Troy will perish, but then he urges Andromache not to mourn: 'No man will hurl me to Hades unless it is fated.' He tells her to go back to the house and do her work and let the men tend to the fighting. But Andromache returns and rouses the other women in the house to a formal lamentation for the dead: 'So they mourned him in the house while he was still living' (500).

So it is primarily from the women that we learn what the men in the epic are like when they are not at war. Helen tells us how kindly Priam has always treated her (*Il*.3.172), and how Hector in the twenty years she has been at Troy never spoke a harsh word to her nor an insult (*Il*.24.767). Briseis tells us how Patroclus reassured her when Achilles killed her husband and brothers; 'You were kind always' (*Il*.19.291-300). By speaking of the kindness and generosity that accompanies even the most terrible violence, the women remind us of the peace war ironically always aims to restore; like the similes that describe shepherds and farmers and forests, they enable us to remember that war is savage and uncivilised as well as grand.

Invariably the women in the *Iliad* remind us of the family ties that are broken by the war. The *Iliad* begins with a description of Chryses seeking to get back his daughter; in *Iliad* 3 Helen wishes she had not forsaken 'her chamber and kinsmen, and my grown child, and the loveliness of girls my own age' (174-5).[4] Andromache reminds Hector of how Achilles killed her father and her seven brothers and took her mother captive, so that her family is now Hector (*Il*.6.413-28). Achilles is playing on a lyre he took from Andromache's city when the embassy comes to visit him in Book 9; Phoenix then tells him his strangely contorted story[5] of the dangers of anger, which caused Meleager's mother to curse her son because he killed her brothers, and of how his wife gets him to return to battle by describing what happens to women and children captured in war. Briseis speaks of how Achilles killed her three brothers and her husband on the same day (*Il*.19.292-4). Each of these stories helps remind us of how war

[3]On the significance of Andromache's advice, see S. B. Pomeroy, 'Andromaque: un exemple méconnu de matriarchat', *REG* 88 (1975) 15-19.
[4]On the role of the *hēlikia*, see esp. C. Calame, *Les choeurs de jeunes filles en Grèce archaïque* (Urbino 1977) I 75-75 (cf. below, ch.7).
[5]On this topic, see M. M. Willcock, 'Mythological paradeigma in the *Iliad*', *CQ* 14 (1964) 141-54.

destroys the family that it is designed to protect.

These scattered histories help establish the full significance for Troy of Hector's death. Again the victor is Achilles; again it is the helpless, the old man Priam, and the women of Troy who interpret for us its significance: Priam will have no protector in his old age or for his dead body; Hecabe will lose the son she nursed herself and her right to mourn for him when he is dead (*Il.*22.58-89). As if to emphasise that this disruption is the *lasting* effect of war, the *Iliad* ends not with a description of debate or of battle, but with funeral lamentations of Hector's kinswomen. His wife Andromache, following the traditional pattern, speaks first:[6] she talks of the life she will lead as a slave, and suggests that her son will also be enslaved or even killed by the Achaeans; his mother, Hecabe, speaks of Achilles' brutality, and of the other sons that he killed; Helen tells of his kindness, when all others reproached her. So the epic ends with reflection on the fate of the victims, not of the victors of the famous war. Earlier in Book 24 Achilles meets with Priam, and speaks of the meaning of their respective losses. But it is the passive victims, the women who cannot take action for themselves, who have the last words.

That the women *speak* tells us not only of the nature of their loss but of their awareness of it. Achilles' final, more temperate conduct, suggests that knowledge, no matter how painful, is somehow valuable and constructive, in spite of its terrible price. Since tragedy concerns the acquisition of knowledge through suffering, I would like to suggest that Homer offered the tragic poets two basic modes of acquiring knowledge: (1) the male pattern of acquiring it actively as the result of causing someone's death like Achilles with Patroclus; (2) the essentially female pattern of acquiring it passively, through observation and through loss. Christian ethics might encourage us to prefer the second, but the *Iliad* and the *Odyssey* seem to suggest that both modes are necessary at once.

Women are so often the central figures of tragedy because they are by nature victims of the traditional values of society. Aeschylus' Clytemnestra and the suppliant maidens take the male hero's destructive course of action to deal with their problems. But it is Electra (and possibly also Hypermestra) the women who act as women were expected to act, who survive to the ends of their trilogies. Antigone is a threat to Creon not only because she disobeys his edict, but because she is a woman who has done something on her own: 'I am not a man; she is a man , if she can have this power without suffering' (484-5). But Sophocles makes it clear that disaster might have been averted had Creon taken Haemon's advice about learning and yielding

[6]M. Alexiou, *The Ritual Lament in Greek Tradition* (Cambridge 1974) 12-13.

to necessity (710ff.), that is, by not acting like a man.

It is interesting to note that when women take decisions in Sophocles' plays it is primarily on behalf of a male relative. Antigone says in her last speech that she buried Polynices because she had no other close male relatives, and would never have another brother now that her parents were dead; her *sister* Ismene doesn't count (904ff.).[7] When Orestes appears to be dead, Electra considers trying to murder Aegisthus herself. In her anger she urges Orestes to strike Clytemnestra twice if he has the strength (1413). She says that like Clytemnestra she is 'evil, and talks too much, and is full of shamelessness' (606-7); but from the beginning of the play she has undertaken to 'practise evil' (309-10) in order to avenge her father. One needs only contrast her opening lines with those of Euripides' Electra, who begins by complaining about having to carry a water pitcher on her head (54ff.); Sophocles' Electra says how she still grieves for her father, and describes how he died (86ff.). Much of the second half of the play is taken up with expression of love for her brother, first in grief for his supposed death, and then in joy at his return. When Antigone speaks out at the end of the parodos of the *Oedipus at Colonus*, she asks them to take pity on her for what she has suffered on her *father's* behalf; at the end of the play she leaves Athens in order to help her *brothers*.[8]

The ancient critics considered Sophocles the most Homeric of dramatists because he used so many stories from the *Iliad* and the *Odyssey* for his plots (*Vit. Soph.* 20). But to judge from the tragedies that survive, the dramatist who seems most interested in suggesting the full potential of the female pattern of experience was Euripides. Of the several dramas Euripides wrote about the Trojan war, two concentrate on Hecabe's fate after the fall of Troy. In the first, the *Hecabe*, Hecabe learns that her daughter Polyxena must be sacrificed to Achilles and then that her son Polydorus has been murdered by the friend to whom he was sent for safe-keeping. Her response to learning of her double loss is both deceitful and violent; she lures her son's murderer into her tent, where she and her women put out his eyes and stab his sons with the pins of their brooches. Sarah Pomeroy remarks that she prefers this Hecabe and Medea, because they do what they set out to do, and take action, like male heroes. But this is to forget that the consequences of such action are also self-destructive: Medea kills her own children, and Hecabe at the end

[7] See esp. R. Just, *Ideas about Women in Classical Athens* (B.Litt.Anthropology, Oxford 1976) 235.

[8] Yet another reason for not excluding 904ff.; for the importance of brothers, cf. also *Scut.*15-16/Hes. fr.195 M.-W. and Bacchyl.5.127ff. Kinship values are also reaffirmed by the action in the *Sept.*; Just (n.7) 238. But cf. R. P. Winnington-Ingram, *Sophocles* (Cambridge 1980) 145.

of the *Hecabe* will be turned into a dog, that is, literally lose her humanity – she has become like her blinded enemy Polymnestor, her son's murderer, who crawls out from the tent on all fours.[9]

Euripides' other play about the fall of Troy, the *Trojan Women*, shows Hecabe as passive observer, commenting on the Greeks' actions, emphasising the senselessness of war. The ending of the *Trojan Women*, with its lamentations first for Astyanax and then for Troy itself, like the speeches at the end of the *Iliad*, concentrates on what has been lost and the suffering to come. The *Hecabe*, by contrast, offers only the impression of lingering anger, as if the *Iliad* had ended with Achilles dragging Hector around the walls of Troy.

The difference between the two Hecabes is that in the second play she and the other victims understand the consequences of violent action. In the *Trojan Women*, the Greek herald Talthybius advises Andromache to give in because her situation is hopeless; resistance on her part would cause further harm; her son's body might be left unburied (724ff.). Talthybius makes his advice more readily acceptable to Andromache by assuring her that giving in will not result in loss of *timē*: 'No one will say you are doing something shameful or hateful' (*oud' aischron ouden oud' epiphthonon se dran*). In this play Hecabe says she has learned from the fall of Troy that happiness is transient, that everything (in her opinion) depends on chance. But the audience has been told at the beginning of the drama that the Greeks who are now victorious will soon be destroyed because of their impiety, and Cassandra has predicted the murder of Agamemnon and sees herself clearly as the agent of justice (457-61). Vengeance in the end will be carried out by the gods, even though Hecabe no longer has confidence in them (469).

It would be tempting to suggest that the *Hecabe* represented a greater confidence in human power possible in the earlier stages of the Peloponnesian war, and that the *Trojan Women*, produced in 415, expressed Euripides' reservations about the Athenians' capture of Melos and their plans for the expedition against Syracuse. But since no victor list survives to help us date the *Hecabe*, I would prefer to think of the two plays as different, and equally frightening, explorations of the same problem, perhaps very close in date. Dramas concern issues of religions, not of politics: they were performed at the festival of Dionysus, whose religion deals with perception and illusion, and the recognition and acceptance of sudden changes in nature or in state.

[9]*Goddesses, Whores, Wives and Slaves* (New York 1975) 109. Cf. Creusa's attempt to kill her son in the *Ion*. On Medea, see esp. B. Knox, *Word and Action* (Baltimore 1979) 306.

But Euripides' portrait of Andromache may suggest that of the two modes he recommends the heroism of acceptance. In the *Trojan Women*, Andromache, while she does not resist the Greeks physically, first suggests that she commit suicide before becoming the concubine of another man.[10] Hecabe dissuades her, for the sake of her son Astyanax. But then when Talthybius announces that Astyanax must be killed, Andromache does not take up her old resolve to kill herself, but speaks out against the Greeks' savagery and barbarism, and the futility of war (774-5). Nothing specific is said in the play about what will happen to Hecabe once she leaves Troy, but Andromache's behaviour suggests that we should in her case also concentrate on her ability to endure and to distinguish right from wrong even in the case of extreme injustice, such as the death of Astyanax, and Menelaus' clemency toward Helen.

Euripides' *Andromache* (whenever it was produced) concerns her life with Neoptolemus, Achilles' son, in Phthia. She has taken refuge at Thetis' shrine, along with her son by Neoptolemus. Neoptolemus' wife Hermione, daughter of Menelaus and Helen, wants to murder her. But because both she and Andromache are women, they must wait for their male relatives to arrive on the scene before anything can happen. But this is a play where the good people win out in the end and the evil people go away, even though they aren't punished. Andromache has every female virtue: loyalty to her husband, willingness to die to save her child, kindness, good judgment, and intelligence. Unlike Hermione, she lacks entirely the usual female vice of jealousy: she describes how as Hector's wife she nursed his bastard children, to make his life 'a little easier'.[11] Her devotion to Neoptolemus is the more remarkable when one considers that he is the son of the man who killed her husband and is himself the brutal murderer of her old father-in-law Priam. In the *Iphigenia in Aulis* Clytemnestra reminds Agamemnon that she too was compelled to marry Agamemnon, who was her first husband's murderer, but her tone is not accepting and obedient like Andromache's.

Andromache's virtue is championed by Achilles' father Peleus, a hero who has less physical strength than moral conviction, gentleness, and a true humanitarian concern for the welfare of

[10]But a vase-painting, perhaps based on the lost epic *Sack of Troy*, shows her about to hit a Greek soldier with a pestle; J. Boardman, *Athenian Red Figure Vases* (London 1975) 232.

[11]Méridier suggests in the Edition Budé that Euripides has Theano's behaviour in mind (*Il*.5.69-71). Perhaps also Andromache is hoping to set an example of generosity for Hermione, who wants to kill Neoptolemus' bastard son; see A. P. Burnett, *Catastrophe Survived* (Oxford 1971) 135-6.

others. While the villains of the play, Menelaus and Hermione, emphasise the importance of old values like blood ties and inheritance laws, Peleus at the end of the play praises the revolutionary idea of marrying for character: 'and shouldn't a man who thinks right marry from honest homes, and give brides to good men and not desire an evil union, not even if he brings a vastly rich dowry to the house?' (1279-83). The wisdom that comes through understanding and acceptance here earns a tangible reward.

The portraits of Andromache and Peleus are examples of a new ethical heroism that one encounters first in the myths of Pindar's victory odes. In Pindar's hands, a hero like Pelops goes about getting divine aid honestly from his ex-lover Poseidon, in order to win his bride.[12] But in the usual version of the story, he bribed his father-in-law's charioteer to get his father-in-law killed in the race, and then rewarded the charioteer by throwing him into the sea. Pindar's new version of the story places great emphasis on the importance of gratitude and on loving concern for family and old friends; these values get consistent stress even in the most painful of Euripides' dramas, and serve as counter-balance to the violence inherent in human nature.[13] Not surprisingly, these qualities are most often found in persons who are by definition powerless, old men, servants, and women who do not violate the conventions of female behaviour.[14]

Acceptable action by women follows the model set by Penelope: the use of intelligence to help a husband or a brother. Helen, held in Egypt while men fight over her wraith in Troy, uses her intelligence to rescue her husband; Iphigenia contrives to save her brother Orestes from rites of human sacrifice in Tauris. Alcestis' dying to save her husband wins such universal approval that she is brought back to life. Euripides portrays her self-sacrifice as a carefully reasoned action. She explains to Admetus and the audience why it is better for her to die; he accepts her arguments against his marrying a 'stepmother for her children' (305).[15] Polyxena in the *Hecabe* is willing to die because she has lost all her male relatives and thus her status and protectors (342ff.); but as she goes to her death she taunts her captors by undoing her dress, baring her breast, and saying to Neoptolemus, 'Here is my breast, strike it, or if you prefer, young man, here is my throat' (*Hec*.562ff.); then she falls, hiding the other

[12]See A. Köhnken, 'Pindar as innovator,' *CQ* 24 (1974) 199-206.

[13]On the importance of forgiveness and friendship in Euripides' dramas, see esp. M. R. Lefkowitz, 'The poet as hero,' *CQ* 28 (1978) 462-3.

[14]For this reason tragic choruses are mostly composed either of old men or of women: see A. Gouldner, *The Hellenic World* (New York 1965) 110-11.

[15]Cf. the similar arguments used by Ion, 607-17.

half of her body from the army's eyes.[16] Her power, like Penelope's, consists of being able to offer and then withhold herself at the last minute.

But if a woman strikes out against the people who have harmed her, she at best attains only the informed isolation that remains for Achilles at the end of the *Iliad*. In the *Bacchae* Agave kills her son Pentheus, thinking he is a lion; her father slowly brings her back to her senses; [17] for a moment they can express their love for one another through their grief. But then they are driven apart for ever into separate exiles. Agave's fate seems more terrifying to us than Medea's because Agave (like Achilles) was not aware of the consequences of her actions, whereas Medea tells us clearly in advance how well she understands what murdering her own children will mean to her. Yet Agave in the end wins our sympathy because of her regret for her actions and her concern for her father. The *Iliad* ends not with Andromache lamenting her own fate but with Helen speaking about Hector. In developing a heroism that expresses concern for others Euripides had Homer's women in mind.

That Euripides seems to advocate traditional roles of behaviour may strike us as surprising, since it has been fashionable to characterise Euripides as an 'ironist'[18] or as an iconoclastic innovator, like Aristophanes in the *Frogs*. Aristophanes has Aeschylus accuse Euripides of setting bad examples for Athenian women by portraying 'harlots' like Stheneboea and Phaedra on the stage.[19] Whatever Euripides' emphasis was in the *Stheneboea* or in his first play about Hippolytus, Phaedra in our *Hippolytus* would seem rather to illustrate painfully the perils of going beyond society's norms. Phaedra understands this herself: 'When this sexual passion first wounded me, I considered how I might best conduct myself. My first idea was to be quiet and keep my sickness hidden . . . Then I thought of trying to conquer my folly by keeping chaste, and third, since it was not possible to win out over my passion, I decided to die – that was the best decision, let no one deny it.' It is, as she goes on to explain, the only way she can preserve her good name and honour, as well as that of her husband and of her children. But as she has also said at the beginning of that same speech: 'We understand what is good and we recognise it, but we don't manage to bring it off in the

[16]Cf. the historical suicides of virgins described in *AP* 7.492 (during the sack of Miletus, 277 B.C.) and *AP* 7.493 (Corinth, 146 B.C.). Cf. also D. M. Schaps, 'Women in war,' forthcoming.

[17]G. Devereux, 'The psychotherapy scene in Euripides' *Bacchae*,' *JHS* 90 (1970) 35-48.

[18]E.g., P. Vellacott, *Ironic Drama* (Cambridge 1975); see below, ch. 12.

[19]Hence the false accusation that Euripides is misogynistic; see esp. Pomeroy, op. cit. 105-7; Lefkowitz, op. cit. 465-6.

end' (*ta chrest' epistamestha kai gignōskomen ouk ekponoumen de*, 380-1). If she had killed herself at that point, and had not let the nurse go off to find a mysterious cure for her sickness, only a limited amount of damage would have been done. But by allowing the nurse to persuade her that one should give in to the forces of desire, she is compelled to take action, by writing the letter that accuses Hippolytus falsely and which results in his death. The play is called *Hippolytus* and not *Phaedra* because he, not Phaedra, manages at the end to accept the injustice done him and not to be angry at his father or at Artemis, who deserts him at the end. Like the women in *Iliad* 24, his last words set the moral tone of the drama. His powerlessness, in effect, gives him a heroine's capability to understand and to forgive.

Women's compassion sets the course of the constructive action in Euripides' *Suppliants*. Theseus, in deliberate contrast to Creon, takes his mother's advice and fights to recover the bodies of the Argive dead, without pursuing any further an unjustified attack on Thebes. When the bodies are about to be burned, Evadne, Capaneus' widow, rushes in and throws herself on her husband's pyre. But her suicide does not elicit the kind of praise Polyxena wins in the *Hecabe*, because it is unnecessary and selfish. She jumps on to the pyre before the eyes of her father Iphis, who has already lost a son (Evadne's brother Eteoclus) in the same war; Euripides turns the audience's attention to Iphis in his bereavement, and to the women and children who are left to mourn. In this case the benefits of continuing to live are made clear by Athena who predicts ex machina that the dead men's sons will return to sack Thebes. As in the *Trojan Women*, Euripides leaves no doubt that the gods ensure that justice will be done.

But self-sacrifice for the public good wins applause, especially in wartime Athens. Here women are able to play a leading role because the traditional religion seems so often to have demanded the death of a female child. Iphigenia at Aulis overcomes her fear of death and offers herself to be sacrificed on the grounds that her one life will prevent the death of many thousands, and that a female life is less valuable in any case than a man's (1368-1401). Her argument about the relative value of female life would not sound so strange to a Greek audience as it does to us: the plots of Menander's comedies testify that girl babies were more frequently abandoned; Anaxagoras (and Aristotle) accepted Athena's argument in the *Eumenides* that the real parent of any child was the father (Anaxag. A 107D-K; *Eum.* 658-61). Iphigenia's speech wins the chorus' approval for its nobility, as well as Achilles' admiration. Praxithea, in the *Erechtheus*, allows her oldest daughter to be sacrificed to save Athens, just as she would willingly have sent off a son to fight for his fatherland (fr. 50 Austin). In the *Heracleidae*, Macaria states that she must sacrifice herself for her fatherland because she could not bear the disgrace if she continued to live after having refused this opportunity for public service (500-34). Virtually the same arguments are presented by Creon's son Menoeceus in the *Phoenissae*, when he sacrifices himself to save Thebes (985-1008); in this case also women's passive heroism sets the model for a man.

The 'advice' Euripides appears to be giving his audience in these dramas concerns the traditional dangers of trying to break established norms, and of fighting against the inevitable. In the *Bacchae* society comes apart because the women leave their looms and shuttles and go off to run wild in groups through the mountains. Pentheus tries to use force rather than persuasion to bring them back and to stop the worship of the new god without waiting to inquire by oracular means whether his action is justified. Everyone loses in the end, even Cadmus, who advocated accepting Dionysus' worship to begin with. But that is the nature of human life as Homer described it in the *Iliad*; women and old men, who must sit on the sidelines, and endure the consequences of the action in the arena, are best able to interpret its meaning, and, as survivors, to demonstrate its consequences. They show us what we as audience must learn from the epic that is sung to us or from the drama that we see performed in the theatre.

2

The Wandering Womb

As my title implies, gynaecology in ancient Greece was not an exact science. That it was not implies no special prejudice against women. In fact, no branch of ancient medicine depended primarily on what we would call empirical evidence. Observable phenomena and deductions from analogy formed the shaky premises on which doctors in the fifth century based many of their diagnoses. Religious scruples apparently prevented human dissection. Nor did the doctors have the instruments they needed to see what constituted and what destroyed human flesh and blood.[1]

Because of the limitations of their methodology, these doctors' understanding of the female anatomy seems to have been based on dissection of other large animals, such as cows, supplemented by the quasi-data provided by existing social norms, such as women's evident physical and mental inferiority. Even when setting up a utopia, Plato has Socrates and his friends begin from the premise that 'we treat the females as weaker and the males as stronger'.[2]

In this chapter I would like to consider the methods used by fourth-century doctors to diagnose and to treat the women's disease hysteria and also to comment, using Greek tragedy as evidence, on how the disease was understood and dealt with by lay people, especially women. I am concentrating on the Hippocratic corpus because it provides the earliest evidence of what remained the dominant attitude toward female anatomy throughout antiquity. In spite of the great advances in medical science made by doctors in Alexandria, and the sensible and humane precepts of a physician like Soranus, the notion persisted that women's minds could be adversely affected by their reproductive tracts.[3]

I am concentrating on hysteria because theories of the disease and

[1]H. von Staden, 'Experiment and experience in Hellenistic medicine,' *BICS* 22 (1975) 184. On deductions from dissection of animals, G. E. R. Lloyd, *Magic, Reason and Experience* (Cambridge 1979) 217.

[2]Plato, *Rep.* V.451e, tr. Shorey.

[3]Cf. how satyriasis, the sexual disease of men, also affects speech and judgment, Aretaeus 2. 12 (Hude).

prescriptions for its cure occupy such a large proportion of the treatises about women. The amount of space devoted to hysteria seems surprising, since in other respects the gynaecological treatises display a concern with improving the quality of the care of women patients. Their very existence of the treatises, as Geoffrey Lloyd has shown in a recent paper, shows that doctors wished to raise the treatment of women's diseases to a medical art, to bring some regulation to home treatment, and to keep women from falling into the hands of unscrupulous practitioners.[4] Dr Lloyd has emphasised the more 'scientific' (in our sense) aspects of Hippocratic gynaecology. I would like to concentrate instead on what Dr Lloyd calls 'fantastical doctrines'; cures that could only be effective because of their symbolic associations, and diagnoses that could be based on analogy rather than on observation. I will suggest that in maintaining that the womb could become dislodged and travel around the body doctors were not concerned so much with physical healing as with upholding the established values of society; hence the 'politics' of my title. I do not mean that a doctor's purpose was more 'political' than that of the woman he treated, since both accepted the notion of the disease's existence. I mean only to argue that the disease hysteria should be regarded like other Greek myths, as representative of certain unquestioned but generally acknowledged 'facts' of human life.

The term hysteria means 'wombiness'; *hysterai*, literally the 'latter parts', is the politely vague term for uterus (medical texts also use the more descriptive *mētrai*, the mothering area). The words usually appear in the plural because doctors had only seen the bicornuate uteri of animals.[5] The social problems caused by this strange, unseen organ are vividly described in the short Hippocratic treatise *About Virgins*.[6] The writer says he is interested in the disease called 'sacred' (epilepsy), and in loss of consciousness (apoplexy) and in 'terrors' in which people see hostile *daimones*, either during the night or the day or both.[7] Like the writer of the treatise *On the Sacred Disease* he believes that such visions are caused by physical disorders:

[4]G. E. R. Lloyd, 'Treatises on women in the Hippocratic corpus,' forthcoming.

[5]M .R. Lefkowitz & M. B. Fant (edd.), *Women's Life in Greece and Rome* (new ed. London 1981) hereafter *WLGR*, s.v. hysteria. On the etymology of *hystera*, see H. Frisk, *Griechisches Etymologisches Wörterbuch* (Heidelberg 1969) s. v.

[6]E. Littré, *Oeuvres Complètes d'Hippocrate* (Paris 1839–61) VIII.466–70 (hereafter L); B. Simon, *Mind and Madness in Ancient Greece* (Ithaca 1978) 266. On problems resulting from menstrual retention, see also I. Veith, *Hysteria* (Chicago 1965) 37–8.

[7]Lloyd (n.1) 28; interrelationship between melancholia (affecting the mind) and epilepsy (affecting the body) is observed in *Epid.* VI. 31/L V. 354.

As a result of such a vision [in the night], many people choke to death, more women than men, for the nature of women is less courageous and is weaker. And virgins who at the appropriate time for marriage do not take on a husband, experience these visions more frequently, especially at the time of their first monthly period, although previously they have had no such bad dreams of this sort. For after the first period the blood collects in the womb in preparatioh to flow out; but when the mouth of the egress is not opened up, and more blood flows into the womb on account of the body's nourishment of it and its growth, then the blood which has no place to flow out rushes up because of its abundance to the heart and to the lungs; and when these are filled with blood, the heart becomes sluggish, and then because of the sluggishness numb, and then because of the numbness insanity takes hold of the woman. Just as when one has been sitting for a long time the blood that has been forced away from the hips and the thighs collects in one's lower legs and feet, it brings numbness, and as a result of the numbness one's feet are useless for movement, until the blood goes back to where it belongs. It returns most quickly when one stands in cold water and wets the tops of one's ankles. This numbness presents no complications, since the blood flows back quickly because the veins in that part of the body are straight, and the legs are not a critical part of the body. But blood flows slowly from the heart and from the *phrenes* (the 'mind', located in or near the lungs).[8] There the veins are slanted, and it is a critical place for insanity, and suited for madness.

One needs to know little human physiology to realise that the evidence in this treatise could not have been collected from experimentation or from physical examination. Instead the doctor has described what he cannot see by analogy with what he can, and by application of abstract logic. One's feet tend to become swollen or numb when one has been sitting down for a long time; this must be caused by accumulation of excess blood from the womb, if the blood has no way to flow down and out; since the mind is located near the heart, it like the feet is adversely affected by the accumulation.

The rest of the treatise describes the dangers of this adolescent hysteria and prescribes a cure:

When these places [the heart and the lungs/mind] are filled with blood, shivering sets in with fevers. They call these erratic fevers. When this is the state of affairs, the girl goes crazy because of the violent inflammation and becomes murderous because of the decay, and is afraid and fearful because of the darkness; they try to choke themselves because of the pressure on their hearts; their will, distraught and anguished because of the bad condition of the blood, forces evil on itself. In some cases the girl says dreadful things: they (the visions) order her to jump up and throw herself into wells and to drown, as if this were good for her and served some useful purpose. When a girl does not have visions, a desire sets in

[8]R. B. Onians, *The Origins of European Thought* (Cambridge 1951) 23ff.

which compels her to love death as if it were a form of good. When this person returns to her right mind, women give to Artemis various offerings, especially the most valuable of women's robes, following the orders of oracles; but they are deceived. The fact is that the disorder is cured when nothing impedes the downward flow of blood. My prescription is that when virgins experience this trouble, they should cohabit with a man as quickly as possible. If they become pregnant, they will be cured. If they don't do this, either they will succumb at the onset of puberty[9] or a little later, unless they catch another disease. Among married women, those who are sterile are more likely to suffer what I have described.

The cure for the problem consists (quite logically) of getting the blood that appears to be causing the trouble to flow out in the right direction. Rather than prescribing a potentially dangerous surgical procedure to open the blocked passage, such as hymenectomy, the doctor offers as a cure social conformity, marriage and pregnancy. The doctor proceeds on the assumption that the causes of mental disorders in young females are in origin sexual; these women are seen first in terms of their reproductive role, and as controlled by their principal reproductive organ. Io in the *Prometheus Bound* is portrayed as a victim of this type of hysteria.[10] She describes how 'visions in the night' have come into her virgin's bedchamber, urging her to go out to the meadow to meet with Zeus, who desires her. But she is frightened and resists; then she is driven from her home, her shape altered, her mind (*phrenes*) 'turned inside-out', horned like a cow, stung (or, literally, 'rubbed') by a gadfly. She comes onstage in a frenzy, uncertain where she is, eager to die: 'burn me with fire, bury me in earth, give me as food to the beasts of the sea'.[11]

In other Hippocratic treatises, the womb itself is said to wander through the body causing trouble, until it can be brought back again to its proper place:[12]

> Whenever in a woman who has never given birth the menses are suppressed and cannot find a way out, illness results. This happens if the mouth of the womb is closed or if some part of her vagina is prolapsed. For if one of these things happens, the menses will not be able to find a way out until the womb returns to a healthy state . . .

Under these conditions 'the womb is displaced'; also if it is not

[9]Fourteen seems to have been average; see D. W. Amundsen and C. J. Diers, 'The age of menarche in Classical Greece and Rome,' *Human Biology* 41 (1969) 125-32; Pomeroy, *GWWS* 23ff.

[10]See esp. J. Dumortier, *Le Vocabulaire médical d'Eschyle et des écrits hippocratiques* (Paris 1935) 69-79.

[11]Aesch., *PV* 645-9, 563-608.

[12]The notion that human wombs were movable may have been deduced from observation of wombs of cows or horses, which may come out after parturition and can be replaced.

sufficiently damp, as in the case of women who do not have intercourse. Also, 'when two months menses are accumulated in the womb, they move off into the lungs where they are prevented from exiting'.[13]

According to the treatises, a dislocated womb that has lodged near a woman's head causes torpor or foaming at the mouth.[14] Sympathetic magic is used to get it back: foul-scented fumigations are placed beneath her nose, and sweet-scented fumigations near her vagina. If the dislocated womb has lodged in a woman's abdomen, it can be lured back by causing her to sneeze and by inserting wool pessaries (i.e., suppositories) in her vagina, which sounds like a medical substitute for the sexual act.[15] If the womb has moved toward her hips, so that her periods stop, the woman is made to eat garlic, and to take a laxative; the doctor puts his finger into the mouth of the womb, then inserts a pessary made of twigs, then a pessary made of opium poppies. If she still has difficulties with her period, she is to eat powder made from cantharid beetles,[16] and to sit in warm water; but the certain cure for this type of dislocation is pregnancy. If the womb moves towards the liver, a problem that in particular afflicts old maids and widows, causing laryngitis, chattering teeth, and darkened colouring, the doctor pushes the womb back down with his hands, and ties a bandage below the woman's ribs to keep the womb from moving up again.

The womb in its wandering behaves like insane women in myth. Euripides in the *Bacchae* describes how the women of Thebes in their madness leave their weaving and go off to run in bands through the mountains, eating off the land, fighting off the men who try to bring them back; their behaviour has been compared to that of oppressed peoples in cults which permit them through ecstasy to enjoy what they lack in ordinary life, control over their environment, and the voice to express themselves.[17] After Agave in a maenadic rage has killed her own son Pentheus, thinking he is a lion, her delusions are dispelled by the patient and skilled questioning of her father Cadmus.[18] Similarly, a male prophet's intervention, in the form of shouting and a ritual dance, is needed to restore the sanity of the wandering daughters of Proetus.[19] Io, wandering, pregnant, with horns like a

[13]*Mul.* I. 2–5/L VIII 14–30, tr. A. Hanson in *WLGR*.
[14]Ibid. II. 123–6/L VIII 266–72; *Nat. Mul.* 2, 3, 8/L VII 312–16, 322–4 in *WLGR*. Cf. Veith (n.6) 10–14.
[15]Simon (n.6) 242–3.
[16]I.e., 'Spanish fly', an irritant still used as an abortifacient.
[17]I. Lewis, *Ecstatic Religion* (Baltimore 1971) 101; Simon (n.6) 252.
[18]G. Devereux, 'The psychotherapy scene in Euripides' *Bacchae*,' *JHS* 90 (1970) 35–48.
[19]Apollod. II. 21; W. Burkert, *Homo Necans* (Berlin 1972) 191–3.

cow, is restored to her normal form and delivered of her child by a touch of Zeus.[20] Male attention, therapeutic or punitive, is needed to restore the insane woman to society, or the dislocated womb to its normal function.[21]

Since both myth and medicine describe a similar pattern of behaviour, the sexual definition of woman's health would seem to predate the founding of Hippocratic science. Thus the doctor's prose only records and sets forth what had been for centuries accepted as truth by all members of society, men and women, patients and doctors. Euripides in the *Hippolytus* describes how *women* diagnose and try to cope with a case of hysteria. At the beginning of the play, Phaedra is described as raving, anorexic, suicidal. The female chorus, on their way back with the clothes they have been washing, suggest that she may be suffering from a female disorder because her husband has been away from her for a long time:[22]

'A miserable helplessness customarily dwells in women's ill-turned structure, a helplessness of labour pains and insanity. This breeze once rushed through my womb, and I called on the heavenly one who brings release, Artemis, mistress of arrows, and she – who is always most admirable – with the gods' grace, comes to me.'

Ambiguous language, 'miserable helplessness' (*dystanos amēchania*), 'ill-turned structure' (*dystropos harmonia*) poignantly expresses the chorus's ignorance of the phenomenon which besets them. The insanity that results from labour pains and mindlessness is a 'breeze' which 'shoots' (*ēiksen*) through their wombs; the same word describes the rushing (*anaïssei*) of the diverted menstrual blood into the heart of the adolescent female. Wind denotes a violent force, externally generated; a problem the woman cannot control or cure by herself: the poet Ibycus compares the violence of passion to the sudden rushing of the north wind.[23]

Anyone who is familiar with the Hippocratic material will suspect that the chorus is describing an attack of hysteria. But the ancient commentary on these lines instead confusingly suggests that the chorus are not talking about themselves but about Phaedra, and that she is worried about getting pregnant as the result of the adulterous

[20]Aesch., *PV* 848-9; the ms. reading *emphrona* may be correct, since she would become sane only by becoming pregnant.

[21]Cf. how St. Irene, who had been living 'on the mountains' was sentenced to a brothel by the Roman prefect; *Acts of the Christian Martyrs*, ed. H. Musurillo (Oxford 1972) 22. v–vi, in *WLGR*.

[22]Eur., *Hipp.* 161-9; W. S. Barrett, ed. (Oxford 1965); Simon (n.6) 258.

[23]Fr. 286. 6–13. Cf. also the 'breeze' (*aura*) that epileptics sense at the onset of an attack, Galen 8. 194 (Kühn).

liaison she is contemplating with Hippolytus.[24] The best modern commentary also speaks of the melancholy of pregnancy, with the suggestion that the 'odd' metaphor of the breeze *may* express unpredictability.[25] But the text emphasises helplessness and its inherence in women's nature. The scholarly editors seem less well attuned to women's problems than Euripides. Here and in other plays he proves to be a particularly sensitive observer of women's thoughts and speech. The remedy Phaedra seeks for her hysteria, but is ashamed to speak of, is not what the doctor recommended for hysterical virgins: intercourse with a husband. A doctor could not have approved when Phaedra's nurse seeks to cure her by trying to get her stepson Hippolytus.

Meanwhile the chorus suggest another course of therapy. In their affliction they sought relief not through their husbands or doctors but from the goddess Artemis, 'the heavenly one who brings release . . . and she comes to me'. That women with female disorders frequently turned to Artemis is clear from the doctor's condemnation of Artemis in the treatise on virgins. 'When this person returns to her right mind, women give to Artemis various offerings, especially the most valuable of women's robes, following the orders of the oracle; but they are deceived.' Artemis' virgin status gives her freedom to come and to go, and to engage in men's pursuits like hunting and being out-of-doors, and travelling to other places.[26]

Marriage marked the time when young women were forced to give up the freedom and the immunity they had enjoyed. That the transition was significant for them is apparent from special rituals to Artmis and goddesses like her. At Brauron in Attica young girls called 'bears', wearing saffron robes, brought Artemis offerings of rabbits, birds, and other wild animals. The girls participated in dance competitions and races; sometimes the girls ran naked, a custom ordinarily reserved for men.[27] In Sparta girls 'anointed like men', with olive oil – that is to say, without clothes on – ran races in honour of Helen, who was worshipped there as a tree goddess.[28]

[24]Scholium to 161, ed. Schwartz.
[25]Barrett (n.21) *ad loc.*
[26]*Hymn. Hom.* 5. 16-20. In Bacchyl. 11. 95ff. Proetus (n.18) prays to Artemis to restore his daughter's sanity.
[27]Ar., *Lys.* 641-7, with scholia; L.-G. Kahil, *Ant.K.* 8 (1965) 20-33; 20 (1977) 86-98; discussion in P. Pearlman, 'Arkteia' (M.A. diss. Berkeley, unpublished). Cf. W. Burkert, *Griechische Religion der archaischen und klassischen Epoche* (Stuttgart 1977) 236-7. Since the girls who participated in the Brauronia were ten years old or younger, the rites may have been concerned with fertility in general rather than specifically with puberty (a particular interest of our own culture); see E. Ardener, 'Belief and the problem of women', *Perceiving Women*, ed., S. Ardener (NY 1975).
[28]Theoc. *Id.* xviii. 21-4; cf. Callim., *Hymn* v. 23-9, with nn. *ad loc.* in A. W. Bulloch, ed. (Cambridge, forthcoming).

The races, dancing, and hunting represent in ritual a stage of life that would no longer be permitted to the girls once they began to bear children.[29] Other aspects of the rituals prepare the girls to come to terms with their new roles as wives and mothers. At Brauron girls carried baskets to the goddess. In the festival Arrhephoria in Athens the girls brought the virgin goddess Athena a chest and a robe they had woven; the myth enacted in the ritual concerns the discovery of a baby surrounded by snakes in a chest or coffin; carrying the robe and basket thus represents the responsibilities of weaving, sex, and child-bearing.[30] As part of the ritual to Helen, women carried baskets containing 'unspeakable holy objects'.[31] A song composed for maidens in Sparta by the male poet Alcman in the seventh century describes a ritual in which girls carry a robe to a goddess. Commentators have been puzzled by the erotic tone of the song; the girls talk of each other's physical beauty, comparing themselves to the leaders of their teams, and the leaders to each other: 'You wouldn't go to Aenesimbrota's house and say, let me have Astaphis, I wish Philylla would look at me, or lovely Damareta, or Vianthemis – it's Hagesichora who excites me.'[32] The girls compare themselves to race horses: 'Don't you see? Agido is a Venetic steed; but my cousin Hagesichora's hair shines like unmixed gold. How can I say it plainly? That's Hagesichora!' Referring to race horses might make particular sense if this song were sung at the same festival in which the girls ran 'anointed like men' in honour of Helen.[33] In the festival for Helen girls compared themselves to the beautiful goddess, while celebrating her marriage to Menelaus. The girls' interest in being beautiful, and not just in being swift runners, may represent the transition from girlhood to womanhood.

It is significant that women turn to a goddess and to celebrations with other women of all ages during these critical periods of physical change. Among themselves they seem better able to express their feelings. According to what women themselves say, it is not sexual desire, but ignorance, fear, and resentment of their prescribed role in life that makes them 'mad'. Euripides portrays Phaedra as telling her

[29]On 'symmetrical reversal' in Greek puberty rites and myth, see P. Vidal-Naquet, 'The black hunter and the origin of the Athenian *ephebia*,' *PCPS* 14 (1968) 49-64.

[30]W. Burkert, 'Kekropidensage und Arrhephoria,' *Hermes* 94 (1966) 1-25.

[31]Pollux x 191; see M. P. Nilsson, *The Minoan-Mycenaean Religion*[2] (Lund 1950) 530. On baskets in ritual, Nilsson, *Griechische Feste* (Berlin 1906) 350-2. Were the 'unspeakable objects' eggs? Paus. saw Leda's egg (!) hanging in the Spartan sanctuary attended by the virgin priestesses the Leucippides, III. 16.1.

[32]Fr. 1, esp. 39-101.

[33]Theoc., *Id.* xvii. 21-4. C. Calame, *Les choeurs de jeunes filles en Grèce archaïque* (Urbino 1977) 119-21, suggests that the goddess to whom they are bearing the robe (61) is Helen, as in Theoc., rather than Artemis Orthia (cf. below, ch.7).

nurse and the women of the chorus that she wishes go go hunting in the mountains, like the Bacchant women of Thebes: 'I have a passion to run with the dogs and to throw my Thracian spear . . .'[34] She may meet Hippolytus there, of course, but she will also escape from the confinement of her household. Medea complains that while a man can go out when he is bored at home, a woman is compelled to 'look to one soul alone', her husband.[35] In a fragment of Sophocles' *Tereus*, Procne, who has been betrayed by her husband, poignantly describes the reasons why the transition from girlhood is so painful:[36]

> But now, outside of my father's home, I am nothing. Young women, in my opinion, have the sweetest existence known to mortals in their father's homes. For their innocence always keeps children safe and happy. But when we reach puberty and can understand, we are thrust out and sold away from our ancestral gods and from our parents. Some go to strange men's homes, others to foreigners', some to joyless houses, some to hostile. And all this once the first night he yoked us to our husband, we are forced to praise and to say that all is well.

A female poet, Erinna, in the fourth century also speaks of the carefree days of play and friendship with her girlfriend in her youth, first cut off by her friend's marriage, and then forever by her friend's early death:[37]

> These traces of you lie still warm in my heart . . . All . . . is now embers . . . We clung to our dolls in our rooms . . . the Bogey Mormo terrified us, with her big ears; but when you went to a man's bed then you forgot everything that you had heard from your mother when you were a baby. Aphrodite . . . oblivion . . .

The author of the Hippocratic treatise *Diseases of Women* comments with sympathy on women's isolation and ignorance:[38]

> These diseases are dangerous . . . and difficult to understand because of the fact that women are the ones who share these sicknesses. Sometimes women do not know what sickness they have until they have experienced the diseases which come from menses and they become older. Then both necessity and time teach them the cause of their sicknesses.

But it was not the doctors, but the poets, students of human emotions, who were better able to perceive that the causes of hysteria

[34]Eur., *Hipp*. 215-22.
[35]Eur., *Med*. 244-8.
[36]Soph., fr. 583 Radt. On Greek marriage rituals in which the husband is portrayed as enemy, see Burkert, *Homo Necans* (n.19) 75.
[37]*Greek Literary Papyri* 120, ed. Page, 11.6-7,12-7. For a different reconstruction and interpretation, see M. L. West, *ZPE* 25 (1977); his arguments are effectively countered by S. B. Pomeroy, *ZPE* 32 (1978) 17-22.
[38]*Diseases of Women* I. 62/L VIII 126 tr. A. Hanson.

were psychological rather than physical; that menarche was not the cause but the signal for a major dislocation in a woman's life; that sexual deprivation offered unwelcome opportunity to reflect on the limitations of one's existence and to worry about one's deviation from established social norms.

While medical treatises emphasised the negative effect of the womb on women's behaviour, popular belief and formalised philosophy denied the womb its basic creative powers. Again the role of women's organs in reproduction was not understood because they could not be seen. It was assumed that conception took place at the beginning of the menstrual cycle, when semen could be sustained in the menstrual fluid (the only visible product of the female reproductive tract). The woman's role in childbearing could thus be perceived fundamentally to be that of receptacle. When in Aeschylus' *Eumenides* Orestes is on trial for murdering his mother, Apollo helps win his case by demonstrating that Clytemnestra was the less important of Orestes' two parents: 'She who is called the child's mother is not its begetter, but nurse of the newly sown conception. The begetter is the male, and she as a stranger preserves the offspring, if no god blights its birth.'[39] Apollo then points to Athena, who is presiding at the trial; she is a goddess who has no mother, since she was born from the head of her father Zeus. According to the traditional story, Zeus swallowed her mother Metis whole, so that she could not bear him a son who would be stronger than himself.[40] Apollo could also have cited the story of how Zeus sewed the embryonic Dionysus in his thigh after he had torn him from his mother Semele's burned body.[41] In these myths a female is needed only initially in order for conception to take place; then a male can take over. The female's role in childbearing is passive, like a fertile field receiving seed and rain, in which without conscious effort or understanding on her part, plants would eventually grow and then be harvested.[42]

The philosophers, with elegant deductive logic, slightly refined this elemental view of women's role in order to account for the fact that children could bear strong physical resemblance to their mothers. Aristotle describes the menstrual fluid as 'semen, not indeed semen in a pure condition, but semen needing to be acted

---

[39]Aesch., *Eum.* 658-61, tr. H. Lloyd-Jones; Pomeroy, *GWWS* 65. Anaxagoras 50 A 107 D-K.

[40]Hes., *Theog.* 886-900.

[41]Eur., *Ba.* 88-98.

[42]Cf. Aesch., fr. 125.20 f. Mette, describing the rain falling on the earth as the model of animal reproduction.

upon'.[43] The mechanics of reproduction thus appear to be deduced from the male's more vigorous role in sexual intercourse: 'Male is that which is able to concoct, to cause to take shape, and to discharge. Female is that which receives the semen, but is unable to cause semen to take shape and to discharge it.' Similarly, if man's physique is held to be the norm, women's appearance by deviating from that norm must be held to be inferior: men go bald; since women do not, this indicates that their nature is closer to children's who have smaller brains than adults and who cannot produce active seminal secretions.[44]

That ancient scientists discovered 'facts' that confirmed their starting premises is not surprising.[45] Modern researchers too find similarly co-operative data, unless careful precautions are taken.[46] But scientific error in ancient medical treatises at least provides evidence of doctors' *attitudes* and their assumptions. The Hippocratic doctors did not challenge the traditional organisation of society, but worked within it.[47] They were further limited by the traditional purview of their training; they treated women's symptoms with external means, medicine and rhetoric.[48] Beginning from clearly defined premises about the world and his art, the doctor speaks with assurance and authority in the face of danger. Names of patients are not mentioned, confidentiality is preserved, symptoms are described generically. Like a philosopher, the doctor presents his conclusions in timeless terms, with abstract nouns; verbs in the present tense, or in conditional clauses of the 'whenever . . . always' type. By setting up a general model, he is able to treat his patients impersonally, as a dramatist uses prehistoric myth to describe the ethics of present-day society.[49]

Also like a dramatist, the doctor describes the exceptional and the dangerous. His view of normality emerges from between the lines and in a conventional form. A woman's good health depends on her serving her basic reproductive function. If married at the conventional age, and with organs in good working order, she becomes pregnant and is successfully delivered, then she will be healthy and happy. But the very existence of doctors argues that such states of being are not easily achieved, and that they are describing an unattainable ideal. One might compare the definition of a happy life

[43]Ar., *de Gen. An.* 728a in *WLGR*.
[44]Ibid., 766a.
[45]See also Lloyd (n.1) 221-2; G. Majno, *The Healing Hand* (Cambridge Mass. 1975) 178.
[46]N. Weisstein, 'Psychology constructs the female,' *Social Education* 35 (1971) 365-6.
[47]The Hippocratic oath gives first priority to payment and support of the doctor's teacher and his family; text in *Hippocrates*, W. H. S. Jones, ed. (London 1923) I 299.
[48]Cf. P. Lain Entralgo, *The Therapy of the Word* (New Haven 1970) 167f.
[49]Simon (n.6) 266; the analogy was first drawn to my attention by Dr R. Padel.

given by the messenger in Euripides' *Bacchae*, after he describes how Agave in her Bacchic frenzy has torn her son to pieces: 'It's best to think straight and to respect the works of gods; I think that is the wisest thing mortals can possess – if they can use it.'[50] The action in the drama preceding his speech, and the agonising scene that follows it, when Agave is made to understand what she has done, implies that few people indeed can accomplish what the messenger describes, and that those few will be happy only if their lives and goals are simple, accepting and unchallenging.

But in the routine day of both doctor and poet, man is beset by forces beyond his control. Euripides has madness come and attack Heracles so that he kills his wife and children; the chorus of the *Hippolytus* pray that passion not attack them, as it has Phaedra, with evil intent nor without due measure; they speak of the breeze of helplessness that darted through their womb.[51] The Hippocratic treatises show the womb, when it does not receive proper attention, as disengaging itself and moving about the body without discernible pattern or intention, causing the person it attacks to behave destructively. Treatment of the disorder involves giving the womb what it wants, to receive seed and to produce offspring; if this is not possible the womb must be appeased with surrogates like pessaries or digital manipulation, or by other sensual rewards, such as perfumes, that will make it want to return. The doctor in being able to advise treatment is more like priest than poet; he explains the nature of the powerful forces beyond man's control, and discovers ways to come to terms with them; like the priest, he will need to convince his patients of the reality of these powers and to believe in them himself, in order to retain his patients' trust and confidence.

Thanks to the technological progress of the last one hundred-and-fifty years, only ancient *attitudes* survive in modern medicine. The notion still prevails that a woman's biological function determines her psychological health. Feminists enjoy quoting Erikson: '(Woman's) somatic design harbours an 'inner space' destined to bear the offspring of chosen men, and with it, a biological, psychological, and ethical commitment to take care of human infancy.' A similar normality is described by Bettelheim: 'We must start with the realisation that much as women want to be good scientists and engineers, they want first and foremost to be womanly companions of men and to be mothers.'[52] The style of these statements bears some resemblance to the ancient medical treatises: authoritative, general,

---

[50]Eur., *Ba*. 1150-2.
[51]Eur., *HF* 861-6; *Hipp*. 521-8.
[52]Cited in Weisstein (n.46) 363.

timeless, more oriented to the needs of society than to the individual. They are pronouncements based on deduction and analogy, not close descriptions of case histories or summaries of accumulated data. By insisting on the primary importance in a woman's life of her biological role, doctors suggest their disapproval of other priorities, such as careers in fields like science and engineering, which take them outside the home and away from husband and family. Because these ambitions constitute a deviation from the norm, they are potentially dangerous, like the continued celibacy that according to the Hippocratic treatise caused hysteria in young virgins or drove Io mad in the *Prometheus* or helped to bring about Phaedra's troubles in the *Hippolytus*.

Similar fears were expressed around the turn of the century, before it was known what effect higher education for women would have upon themselves and upon society. G. Stanley Hall, Professor of Psychology and Paedagogy and President of Clark University, in a widely read book on adolescence began his discussion of women's education with a description of the female anatomy: 'Her organs occupy a larger proportion of her body . . . (they) are hidden and their psychic reverberation dim, less localised, more all-pervasive. She works by intuition and feeling.'[53] Hall showed how intensive courses of study and institutions like Wellesley and Bryn Mawr tend to produce dysmenorrhea and concomitant nervous disorder; he presents several anonymous case histories. He deduced from the limited statistics then available (he had in most cases information about fewer than twenty years of graduating classes) that infertility increased as the level of women's education rose. He suggested that bachelor women, with all their admirable intellectual attainments, tend to develop an intense fear of childbearing.

As an alternative Hall proposed that women attend men's colleges, but that they study subject matters related to what they would do in their homes and to what they would be able to teach their children. Thus Greek, Hebrew, and possibly also even Latin were to be excluded, along with higher mathematics. Marriage should take place in a woman's early twenties, to prevent 'lassitude' and homosexuality. Being educated with men would encourage women to raise the standards of their work in a 'more normal environment', where, it might also be noted, they would have opportunity to meet eligible men.

It is interesting that Hall was not so much afraid of education for

[53]*Adolescence: its Psychology* (New York 1904) 561-647. Cf. also the case histories described in Dr E. H. Clarke's *Sex in Education* (1873), cited in A. M. Wells, *Miss Marks and Miss Woolley* (Boston 1978) 5-9.

women as of single-sex education. Hall had explicit reservations about the vigorous, 'masculine' curriculum of M. Carey Thomas's Bryn Mawr.[54] But one senses that he feared also that women in those colleges might develop for other women the intense ties of affection that they ought to reserve for men; that communities of women, self-governing and self-sufficient, constituted a threat to society – one reflects how many Greek heroes considered it their duty to do battle with the Amazons. Hall speaks disapprovingly also of the 'old traditions' of the type practised in women's colleges. Ceremonies like Bryn Mawr's May Day or Wellesley's Tree Day (cf. below, ch.16) seem harmless enough, but although based on old fertility rites they are enacted entirely by women: Wellesley's Tree Day Mistress and her court of girls made their processional on to the green; there was dancing and a cheerfully competitive parade of the college classes in distinctive colour and costume; a tree was planted, marking for succeeding generations the identity of a class. Nothing was done in the ceremony to anticipate the role of wife and mother that the college woman would most likely later assume.

Hall's fears for society of course have not been realised. Education has only postponed marriage and childbearing. Since the 1930s the proportion of Ph.D.s earned by women has decreased.[55] As Plato foresaw, the structure of society needed to be altered before most women could radically change the course of their existence, and higher education was only one of a number of ways in which women would be enabled to follow what he called 'the same way of life as men'.[56] Plato may have been better able to realise how much adjustment was needed because unlike the doctors he did not begin his consideration of women's role on the basis of women's physiology. Instead he started by commenting on the restrictions of her position in society, and the effect her political and social position had upon her sense of responsibility. Modern doctors in commenting on women's role appear to have been asking more of their medical training, with its anatomical orientation, than it could reasonably deliver. Inscriptions tell us that ancient women went to the shrine of Asclepius at Epidaurus to ask for specific cures to specific physical problems, like a five-year pregnancy.[57] They did not ask (and the god did not give them) approval or assurance about other aspects of their lives.

[54]R. Frankfort, *Collegiate Women* (New York 1977) 87.
[55]Ibid., p.102.
[56]Pl., *Leg*. 806d ff. in *WLGR*.
[57]*IG* IV[2] 121-2 in *WLGR*.

3

Men and Women on
Women's Lives

Since men did most of the writing in the ancient world, it is only natural that most documents speak of the role of women from a man's point of view. Womanly virtues consist of being a supportive wife, a kind mother; respectable women in fourth-century Athens were usually not called by their own names but were known functionally as the wife or daughter of a male relative.[1] Grave inscriptions provide a record of the qualities men conventionally praise. If we compare these eulogies with what women writers wrote about their lives, we can immediately see that women could speak of feelings and experiences that apparently did not matter so much to men.

The documents under the heading 'Praise' in *Women's Lives in Greece and Rome* offer a catalogue of the qualities that men admire.[2] The famous second century B.C. epitaph for Claudia, after praising her beauty, her love for her husband, and her giving birth to two sons, concludes with reference to her demeanour and her housework:[3]

> Friends, I have not much to say; stop and read it. This tomb, which is not fair, is for a fair woman. Her parents gave her the name Claudia. She loved her husband in her heart. She bore two sons, one of whom she left on earth, the other beneath it. She was pleasant to talk with, and she walked with grace. She kept the house and worked in wool. That is all. You may go.

In the Empire, women with professional careers are praised first for their service to family and home. A doctor's husband writes of his wife:[4]

[1] D. Schaps, 'The woman least mentioned,' *CQ* 27 (1977) 323–30.
[2] All texts cited in this chapter appear in *WLGR*. Translations, unless otherwise noted, are my own.
[3] Degrassi I² 973/*CIL* I.2.1211/Dessau 8403; tr. R. Lattimore, *Themes in Greek and Latin Epitaphs* (Urbana 1942).
[4] H. Pleket, *Epigraphica* II (Leyden 1969) no.20.

Farewell, lady Panthia, from your husband. After your departure, I keep up my lasting grief for your cruel death. Hera, goddess of marriage, never saw such a wife: your beauty, your wisdom, your chastity. You bore me children completely like myself; you cared for your bridegroom and your children; you guided straight the rudder of life in our home and raised high our common fame in healing – though you were a woman you were not behind me in skill. In recognition of this your bridegroom Glycon built this tomb for you. I also buried here the body of [my father] immortal Philadelphus, and I myself will lie here when I die, since with you alone I shared my bed when I was alive, so may I cover myself in ground that we share.

To say that his wife bore him children like himself is not so much gratuitous self-praise as a document of his wife's chastity.[5] 'Though you were a woman,' however condescending it sounds, reminds the reader of how unusual her professional accomplishments were. But the husband manages to mention himself in almost every line of the inscription and concludes by testifying to his own fidelity. The epitaph celebrates the partnership more than the individual to whom it is addressed. One can compare the tone of another doctor's epitaph:[6]

You have rushed off to the gods, Domnina, and forsaken your husband, purifying your body with the heavenly stars. No mortal man will say that you have died, but that since you saved your country from diseases the gods stole you away. Farewell and be happy in the Elysian fields. But you have left your friends pain and eternal lamentations.

Only the phrase 'having forsaken your husband' acknowledges the inscription's donor; Admetus, with less justification, complains as his wife Alcestis is dying, 'You are betraying me.'[7] But again Domnina's husband praises his wife for her service to others, and the epitaph concludes with primary reference to them.

The characteristics of men's praise are dramatically illustrated in a long epitaph of the third century A.D. to Allia Potestas, a concubine owned by two men:

To the gods of the dead [the tomb] of Aulus' freed-woman, Allia Potestas. Here lies a woman from Perugia. None was more precious than she in the world. One so diligent as he has never been seen before. Great as you were you are now held in a small urn. Cruel arbiter of fate, and harsh Persephone, why do you deprive us of good, and why does evil triumph?

[5]Cf. the Pythagorean treatise on chastity: 'The greatest glory a freeborn woman can have – her foremost honour – is the witness her own children will give to her chastity towards her husband, the stamp of likeness they bear to the father whose seed produced them.' H. Thesleff, *Pythagorean Texts* (Abo 1965) 151ff. Also Hes. *Op*. 235; 61.214.

[6]Pleket (n.4), no.26.

[7]Euripides, *Alc*. 391.

everyone asks. I am tired of answering. They give me their tears, tokens of their good will. She was courageous, chaste, resolute, honest, a trustworthy guardian. Clean at home, sufficiently clean when she went out, famous among the populace. She alone could confront whatever happened. She would speak briefly and so was never reproached. She was first to rise from her bed and last to return to her bed to rest after she had put each thing in its place. Her yarn never left her hands without good reason. Out of respect she yielded place to all; her habits were healthy. She was never self-satisfied and never took liberties. Her skin was white, she had beautiful eyes, and her hair was gold. An ivory glow always shone from her face – no mortal (so they say) ever possessed a face like it. The curve of her breasts was small on her snow-white bosom. And her legs? Atalanta's figure is comic beside hers. In her anxiety she did not stay still but moved her smooth limbs, beautiful with her generous body; she sought out every hair. Perhaps one might find fault with her hard hands; she was content with nothing but what she had done for herself. There was never a topic which she thought she knew well enough. She remained virtuous because she never committed any crime. While she lived she so guided her two young lovers that they became like the examples of Pylades and Orestes: one house would hold them both and one spirit. But now that she is dead they will separate, and each is growing old by himself. Now instants damage what such a woman built up; look at Troy to see what a woman once did. I pray that it be right to use such grand comparisons for this lesser event. These verses for you your patron – whose tears never end – writes in tribute. You are lost, but never will be taken from his heart. These are the gifts he believes the lost will enjoy. After you no woman can seem good. A man who has lived without you has seen his own death while alive. He carries your name back and forth on his arm, where he can possess it: Potestas is borne on gold. As long as these published words of ours survive, so long will you live in these little verses of mine. In your place I have only your image as solace; this we cherish with reverence and lavish with flowers. When I come to you it follows in attendance. But to whom in my visiting can I trust a thing so venerable? If there is ever anyone to whom I can entrust it, I shall be fortunate in this alone now that I have lost you. But woe is me – you have won the contest – my fate and yours are the same. The man who tries to harm this tomb dares to harm the gods: this tomb, distinguished by its inscription, believe me, has divinity.

The opening and closing lines, more than half the inscription, talk about the donors and describe their reactions to and reflections on Allia's death. As for Allia herself, the owners give extravagant praise to her physical appearance, but they also praise her work in the home. The epitaph for the 'beautiful' patrician Claudia concluded: 'She kept the house; she worked in wool.' Detail makes Allia seem more real but less elevated, almost like a child. She is not valued for her wisdom or her conversation; she strives incessantly to please.

A tense existence surely, threatened by relapse into bad habits: 'She remained virtuous because she never committed any crime'; a life with only temporary value: 'Now instants damage what such a woman built up.' If Allia accomplished or experienced anything apart from her service to her owners or to her household, it is not recorded in her epitaph.

Women's epitaphs for women tend to place more emphasis on the dead woman's own feelings, her relation to her parents, and to her female friends:[9]

> I weep for Antibia, a virgin. Many suitors wanted her and came to her father's house, because she was known for her beauty and her cleverness. But deadly Fate sent all their hopes rolling away.

> Column and my sirens, and mourning urn, you hold me in death, these few ashes. Tell all who pass by my tomb to greet me, be they from this city or another country: 'The tomb holds a bride, my father called me Baucis, I came from Tenos,' so they will know. And tell them that my friend Erinna inscribed this epigram on my tomb.

Women's poetry speaks of loneliness, of the separation caused by marriage as well as by death, of women who leave their women friends for men:[10]

> The man seems to me strong as a god, the man who sits across from you and listens to your sweet talk nearby and your lovely laughter – which, when I hear it, strikes fear in the heart in my breast. For whenever I glance at you, it seems that I can say nothing at all but my tongue is broken in silence, and that instant a light fire rushes beneath my skin, I can no longer see anything in my eyes and my ears are thundering, and cold sweat catches hold of me, and shuddering hunts me all over, and I am greener than grass, and I seem to myself to be little short of death. But all is endurable, since even a poor man . . .

The woman narrator in this influential poem by Sappho compares her weakness to the man's power, but what she describes takes place only in her *imagination*: 'The man *seems* to me' (*phainetai* 1); 'I seem to be little short of death' (*phainomai* 16). In the poem, time, identity, and tangible reality do not matter; the focus is on what the narrator suffers because of her passion. Erinna in her long hexameter poem the *Distaff* writes about a girlhood spent with a now dead friend, of a children's game played: 'These lie in my heart . . . warm traces . . . embers now.'[11] But marriage and then death separated the two friends: 'Dear Baucis, Aphrodite set oblivion on your heart, and so lamenting for you . . . I leave behind.'

[9]Epigrams by Anyte (*AP* vii 490) and Erinna (*AP* vii 710).
[10]Sappho 31; on interpretation, see below, ch.9.
[11]*Greek Papyri* (LCL) III 120; on interpretation, see S. Pomeroy, 'Supplementary notes on Erinna,' *ZPE* 32 (1978) 17-22.

Women's love for one another and the world they share apart from men are not aspects of life described in ordinary poetry. Such intense feelings are voiced only by women in tragedy on the verge of disaster, like Deianeira, Medea, or Procne.[12] Modern male scholars sometimes seem to want to mitigate the force of these feelings. Page translates away Sappho's most forceful language, replacing 'strikes fear' with the passive 'a-flutter', 'thundering' with 'humming', 'greener than grass' with 'paler'. By translating 'when I look at you a moment' rather than 'whenever', he transforms the imaginary and timeless into the particular and real.[13] West proposes supplements to the fragmentary papyrus manuscript of Erinna's *Distaff* that make Erinna in her poem regret not a lost childhood with her friend but her own failure to move from a woman's world into the happier state of marriage; he further proposes that the language of the poem is too sophisticated to have been written by a woman from a small island and suggests that it was a forgery composed by a man: 'What a pity the poet had to conceal his name.'[14] But this is only speculation; *prima facie*, a woman wrote the poem.[15] What women like Procne or Deianeira are given to say about the violent transformation from childhood to marriage suggests that women will be much more likely to lament lost friendships than their failure to acquire husbands.[16]

Christian women too, had more of their words been preserved, might have spoken of the opportunity the new religion gave them to live in communities that did not separate women from each other or even from men. The one first person narrative that has survived testifies to the political and psychological value for women of the Christian faith.[17] In the process of her conversion and in preparation for her martyrdom, Perpetua of Carthage becomes increasingly less encumbered by her femininity. She gives up her baby to be cared for by others: 'As God willed the baby had no further desire for the breast, nor did I suffer any inflammation.' She dreams that she is contending in single combat, and that she is transformed for that purpose into a male:[18] 'My clothes were stripped off and suddenly

[12]Sophocles, *Trach*. 144–50; *Med*. 241ff.; Sophocles, fr. 583 Radt, above, p.20.
[13]See above, pp.63–4.
[14]M. L. West, 'Erinna', *ZPE* 25 (1977) 95–119.
[15]Pomeroy, 'Erinna' (n.11).
[16]Cf. n.12. The transition is marked also by rites of passage; see W. Burkert, 'Kekropidensage und Arrhephoria,' *Hermes* 94 (1966) 1–25; above, pp.18–19.
[17]Acts of the Christian Martyrs, ed. H. Musurillo (Oxford 1972) no.8; for interpretation, see below, ch.8. On the role of women in the early church, see E. H. Pagels, 'What became of God the Mother?' *Signs* 2.2 (1976) 293–303; Averil Cameron, '"Neither Male nor Female"', *G & R* 27 (1980) 60–8.
[18]Only men competed nude and rubbed down with olive oil; cf. Theoc. xvii 21–4, Callim. *Hymn* 5.23–9; above, p.18. Cf. Artemidorus I.30,50 on dreams of acquiring male characteristics.

I was a man. My seconds began to rub me down with oil (as they are wont to do before a contest). Then I saw the Egyptian on the other side rolling in the dust.' She wins her victory by trampling on the Egyptian's head. 'I realised that it was not with wild animals that I would fight, but with the Devil, but I knew that I would win the victory.' But the Egyptian rolling in the dust also resembles her own father, who has been thrown to the ground and beaten with rods when he tried to interrupt her trial and who again threw himself on the ground before her in a final attempt to make her renounce her religion; ' . . . my father was so angered by the word "Christian" that he moved towards me as though he would pluck my eyes out. But he left it at that and departed, vanquished along with his diabolical arguments.'

In contrast to her father's violent opposition, kindly male deacons help her through the trials of prison and the dream contest: '[Pomponius] took my hand and we began to walk through rough and broken country'; 'the trainer kissed me and said to me: "Peace be with you, my daughter!"'.' Like the suicide who believes that he is killing only some part of himself, Perpetua saw martyrdom as the beginning of a new life in which she could determine the course of her own existence, cut herself off from old emotional ties, and win the approval of others than her immediate family. Conventional prayers and homilies are absent from her narrative, as if the standard articles of faith were less immediately important than the opportunity her faith gave her to break away from the social role and the attitudes that had been expected of her. Her father tried to persuade her by calling her *domina* ('woman') instead of *filia* ('daughter'); she herself prefers the name of 'Christian'.

I have tried to suggest by these few examples that women themselves speak of emotions and of shared experiences that appear to have been unknown to many men. Our assessment of ancient values will be more accurate if we begin to give proportional attention to the few women's voices that survive, and if we can listen accurately to what they say. If ancient women had written as much as men, our impression of what mattered in the world would be greatly altered: conversation might count more than physical appearance, punishment be more often internalised, and greater stress be placed on the effect of one's actions on others.

4

Invective against Women

If Cicero's *Pro Caelio* still strikes us as a particularly persuasive speech, a major reason may be its topic: the licentious behaviour of a notorious woman, Clodia.[1] Cicero portrays her as the antithesis of the ideal Roman *matrona*; in particular, he contrasts the behaviour of a 'hypothetical' woman who 'resembles' Clodia (49) with Clodia's second-century ancestress Claudia, for whom the famous epitaph was written. Both Claudia and Clodia are beautiful, but there the resemblance stops.[2] The ancestress Claudia first of all loves her husband with all her heart; Claudia's hypothetical analogue is first of all 'not married'; she 'locates herself openly in a meretricious life'; she holds dinner parties with male *strangers* (the plural of course suggests the life of a prostitute). The *matrona* Claudia bore two children; the *meretrix* Clodia's children are not mentioned; the good Claudia spoke elegantly and walked gracefully; Cicero speaks of Clodia's 'carriage' (*incessus*) and 'finery' (*ornatus*) and 'retinue' (*comitatus*): her entrances claim attention, like the meretrix Erotium's in Plautus' *Menaechmi*, as a good woman's should not.[3] The *meretrix* Clodia not only speaks, but flashes her eyes. The matrona 'kept her house; she worked in wool'. Clodia doesn't stay at home; she is 'in town', 'in her gardens', in Baiae.

But one need not have the epitaph of Claudia in mind to understand why this short passage from the *Pro Caelio*, even removed from its context, is such an effective piece of invective. Hellenistic Greek and Roman epitaphs proclaim virtues similar to Claudia's, and with the same emphases. One of the most remarkable is the epitaph for Allia Potestas, a woman jointly owned by two men.[4] Although Allia Potestas was by definition a meretrix, prized for her beauty and for her body, which they describe in some detail, she is also endowed on her tombstone with the qualities of a matrona: 'she

[1] See esp. K. A. Geffcken, *Comedy in the Pro Caelio* (Leiden 1973) 28ff.
[2] Tr. Lattimore; above, p.26.
[3] Geffcken 30–1; R. G. Austin, ed., *M. Tulli Ciceronis Pro Caelio Oratio*[3] (Oxford 1959) 110.
[4] Above, pp.27–8.

would speak briefly and so was never reproached (*exiguo sermone*: like Claudia's *sermone lepido* 'she was pleasant to talk with'); 'there was never a topic she thought she knew well enough'. 'She was first to rise from her bed and last to return to her bed to rest after she had put each thing in its place. Her yarn never left her hands without good reason.' Claudia 'kept the house, worked in wool' *domum servavit, lanam fecit*. The description of her 'carriage' is more ambiguous but still remarkably dignified for a professional meretrix:[5] 'she was courageous, chaste, resolute, honest, a trustworthy guardian; clean at home, sufficiently clean when she went out, famous among the populace'.

Even a woman physician like Panthia gets praise first for her service to her husband Glycon: 'Hera goddess of marriage never saw such a wife, your beauty, your wisdom, your chastity. You bore me children completely like myself; you cared for your bridegroom and your children.'[6] Claudia 'loved her husband with all her heart; she bore two children'. Only after Panthia's excellence as a wife and mother does husband mention her achievements as a physician: 'You raised high our common fame in healing; though you were a woman you were not behind me in skill.' In the longer inscriptions details help the women stand out more as individuals, as for example in the splendid eulogy of Turia by her husband, which tells of her courageous service to her parents and to him.[7] But since the same emphases on monogamy, children, loyalty to home occur over and over in diverse memorials of all types and from all localities we can be sure that Cicero's description of Clodia struck in his audiences basic resonances indeed.

Since the ideal housewife is praised first for her loyalty to her husband and her bearing of her children, first emphasis in invective against women falls on sexual promiscuity. Since next, and closely related to the first, is the ideal matrona's interest in her home, the meretrix will be characterised as inattentive to household details or even absent altogether. Cicero constantly stresses both these themes in the *Pro Caelio*. He summons up Clodia's ancestor Appius Claudius to ask first 'What business did you have with Caelius . . . a man not out of his teens, a man not your husband,' not a relative or a friend of her husband, a stranger to the house (33). The difference in their ages further implies that she is a professional meretrix, like the sex-starved aging Lydia in Horace, *Odes* 1.25, on the lookout for

[5]E. Fraenkel, 'Two poems of Catullus,' *JRS* 51 (1961) 46-9 on Cat. 42.7-8 'walking disgracefully' (*turpe incedere*).
[6]Above, p.27.
[7]In *WLGR*.

young men.[8] Significantly, Cicero has Appius conclude his tirade by making her adulteries plural (25ff.): 'Did I bring in the Appian Aqueduct that you might put its waters to your dirty uses? Did I build the Appian way that you might ride up and down with other people's husbands?' Catullus speaks in a poem addressed to Caelius of 'that Lesbia, whom he loved more than himself or all his family, now in the crossroads and narrow alleys peels back the descendants of Remus'(58). Note that both Cicero's Clodia and Catullus' Lesbia (whether or not they are in fact the same person) in these invectives take on a plurality of men (in Catullus 11 it is three hundred at once) *outside* their homes.

Cicero uses the same basic line of attack in a second speech in the *Pro Caelio*, in which he pretends to be Clodia's brother Clodius – 'You saw a young man nearby.' She tries to buy him with gifts (again reversing the accepted pattern of behaviour), but since he spurns her Clodius advises her to go after someone else.' 'You have your gardens on the Tiber. You deliberately chose them for their location, since they are at the very place where all the young men go swimming . . . ' (36). Again there is a movement from singular to plural, from the home to the dangerous world outside. To this is added at the beginning of the speech a not very subtle suggestion that Clodia and Clodius have committed incest.

By the time the oration is half over, Cicero has turned the *Pro Caelio* into the *In Clodiam* (49): 'I am not saying anything new, but if there were someone, not the same as she, you understand, some woman who made herself cheap and easy to approach, who always had some man or other hanging about . . . in whose gardens and home and place at Baiae [her *home* is now listed among the places outside] . . . who even boarded young men and paid them . . . If this person, being widowed, lived loosely, being forward, lived wantonly, being rich, lived extravagantly, being prurient, lived like a harlot, should I think a man an adulterer if he did not address her as a matrona?'

Cicero knew that audiences need to be told a thing several times in order to remember it and for this reason surely his orations make better hearing than reading. But in the *Pro Caelio* variation of style and detail keep interest and enjoyment high. A few facts, skilfully deployed, gain significance by being turned into examples of eternal vices: gardens by the Tiber, innocent in themselves, are with Baiae the dangerous outside; a single lover soon becomes a nameless group of assignations.

Cicero's grasping of the essentials of invective and his elaborate

[8]A gap in age always suggested suspicious motives; see Menander, fr.333 in *WLGR*.

exploitation of his knowledge enables us better to understand why less consciously articulated documents are none the less effective. Feminists cite Semonides of Amorgos' poem about women as a prime example of Greek misogyny.[9] Yet Cicero's manner of dealing with Clodia indicates that Hugh Lloyd-Jones is right in interpreting Semonides' poem both as invective and as an entertaining satire.[10] The poem begins by saying that Zeus made for women a mind (*nous*) different from men's, which the poet then explains by analogy. As in Cicero's invective, characterising by type both clarifies and 'reifies'. In the *Pro Caelio* Clodia ceases to be an individual woman living at a particular time and turns into an archetypal meretrix. In Semonides women are no longer human beings but animals or things. Sophocles shows Creon in the *Antigone* using metaphor to remove himself from ordinary concerns of country and of family. The city is a ship (190); Antigone is like steel over-refined and broken (473ff.); Ismene is a viper sucking his blood (531ff.); there are other women's fields for his son to plow if Antigone dies (569ff.). In his speech against Verres, Cicero makes the most out of his victim's name: *verrem* (pig), *verrere* (sweep); *ius Verrinum* (hog gravy).

But Semonides concentrates on how his animals, and earth and sea, behave as *housewives*. As for the women in the epitaphs, emphasis falls on their conduct in the home. The pig-woman (2ff.) is of course dirty; the fox woman can't distinguish between good and bad (7ff.); the earth-woman is ignorant (21ff.) and so unresponsive that she won't move near the fire in the winter; the bitch-woman snoops into everything (14ff.), 'always yapping . . . a man cannot stop her by threatening, nor by losing his temper or by knocking out her teeth with a stone';[11] cf. the praise on Claudia's epitaph for her *sermo lepidus*. The sea-woman is alternately happy and violent, unpredictably (27ff.).

But in the second half of his list Semonides begins to talk explicitly about sexual conduct. The donkey woman works and eats continually (43ff.), 'and likewise when she comes to the act of love she accepts any partner' (48-9). The weasel-woman is 'ugly, displeasing, thieving, and impious', but also 'mad for the bed of love, but she makes any man who is with her sick' (53-4). The horse-woman (57ff.) is lazy, an expensive luxury, always taking baths and putting on perfume. The monkey woman (71ff.) is the worst plague of all because she is ugly, shameless, plans harm for people, and – it is implied – no pleasure to have in bed. As for Clodia, sexual promiscuity

[9]Cf. Pomeroy *GWWS* 49: 'the hostility of Hesiod is reiterated by Simonides'.
[10]*Females of the Species* (London 1975) 22-9; below, ch.11.
[11]Tr. Lloyd-Jones, in *WLGR*.

and shamelessness are linked; the good matrona provides no cause
for gossip: 'the whole neighbourhood reeks of nothing else; people
gossip of nothing else; Baiae itself talks about nothing else – not just
talks but reverberates that this one woman's sensuality has gone so
far that she seeks neither solitude nor shadows and such coverings
for her disgraceful acts, but enjoys herself in the most disgusting
actions with constant notoriety and with the most brilliant
illumination'(47).

In both Semonides and the *Pro Caelio* there is a consistent emphasis
either on the women's unresponsiveness toward others or their
outright selfishness, like the horse-woman who ignores the house
but spends all day taking care of herself. Clodia in addition to her
other faults is self-serving and self-indulgent; she wants men for
herself, and buys them with presents. Compare Allia Potestas who
took care to seek after and remove every hair on her smooth limbs,
but whose day did not end until the house was properly seen to.

Semonides' list is brought to an end by an antithesis, a description
of a good woman, who is compared to a bee (83ff.): 'The man who
gets her is fortunate, for on her alone blame does not settle. She
causes his property to grow and increase, and she grows old with a
husband whom she loves and loves her, the mother of a handsome
and reputable family.' As in the epitaphs of Claudia and Panthia, this
woman is praised first for her service to her husband. Then follows
specific reference to her uniqueness, beauty, and chastity: 'She stands
out among all women, and a godlike beauty plays about her. She
takes no pleasure in sitting among women in places where they tell
stories about sex. Women like her are the best and most sensible
whom Zeus bestows on men.'

The poem continues with further reflections on how frequently
husbands fail to perceive how their wives are unfaithful to them, and
breaks off with a reference to the men who died fighting for a
woman in the war against Troy. As in the epitaphs for Claudia,
Panthia and Allia Potestas, women are praised for their service to
men; evil women are distinguished by their selfishness. Semonides'
emphasis on service helps us see yet another reason why Cicero's
characterisation of Clodia was so devastating, at least before a jury
composed of men. A man insults a woman for her deficiencies in
respect to *men*: Archilochus tells the girl he is trying to seduce that he
prefers her to Neobule because she 'has lost the bloom of girlhood;
she's mad and can't restrain herself'; her infidelity would make him a
laughing-stock (PCol. 7511. 23, *charma*). Euripides has Hermione
blame Andromache for using witchcraft to make her infertile, and
for promiscuity – she sleeps with and has borne a child to the son of

the man who killed her husband: 'that's the way foreigners are; fathers mate with daughters and sons with mothers and girls with brothers' (*And.* 171ff.). Andromache replies by explaining how a woman should serve and comply with her husband (222). But women among themselves may not always have taunted each other about their *men*. Sappho criticises her analogue Andromeda for being captivated by a 'yokel' girl who 'doesn't know how to gather her rags about her ankles' (57.3).[12]

The greater restraint of the *In Caecilium* and the First Verrine oration may indicate that ridicule is most effectively employed when one's adversary is powerless or even absent. Women in particular or in general thus make ideal subjects for pleasurable abuse. We will be mistaken if we take Semonides' poem more seriously than Cicero's attack on Clodia. But the special emphases in these invectives can remind us of one of the major problems of writing the history of women in the ancient world: most of our documents are by men. Since men do the talking and the writing women tend to be defined and described in their relation to *men*, and not as they would speak to themselves or to each other. Hence, I think, in the invectives against women, the consistent emphasis on selfishness and on sex, or, in Juvenal's case, special satirising of the women who try to act like men: the woman gladiator who puts down her armour when she uses the chamber-pot (264); the woman with 'dried-up breasts' who is interested in politics (401), or the woman who discourses on poetry (434ff.). Invective against men covers a wider range of subjects: drunkenness, gluttony, pretentiousness, avarice, bad social background, eccentricity of dress.[13] Antony in the Second Philippic indulges in sexual excess with Cytheris, but Cicero (and Caelius, too) also call attention to his drunkenness and vomiting. But in the *Pro Cluentio*, the most telling criticism of Cluentius' mother Sassia is her 'unnatural' lust for her son-in-law. Ilona Opelt's list of invective terms against women concentrate on their dangers to men: witch, poisoner, but particularly *stimulatrix*, ruin, enticement, destruction, criminal, evil, cunt.[14] The first 'case history' in Juvenal's Sixth Satire is Eppia, who left her husband for a gladiator ('It's the sword they're in love with,' 112). The next is Messalina, who leaves her emperor husband at night to work in a brothel, is the last to leave, and still isn't satisfied (128ff.).

Since in Semonides' day women were not involved in work outside

[12]But cf. Praxilla 754.
[13]R. G. M. Nisbet, ed., *M. Tulli Ciceronis In Pisonem Oratio* (Oxford 1961) 194-7.
[14]*Die lateinischen Schimpfwörter und verwandte sprachliche Erscheinungen* (Heidelberg 1965) 106-9. On Greek women, see also Just (p.5, n.7) 250ff.

the home or farm, it is not surprising that praise or blame of women primarily concerns marriage and family. In Hellenistic times and after, as Sarah Pomeroy has shown, more women were (honourably) employed outside the home.[15] Yet even so praise, as for Panthia, and blame constantly refer to their biological roles. Praise and blame for men, understandably, deals with their accomplishments in the outside world where they spend most of their time, and in which their success is measured. Exceptions to the rule are eulogies for young virgins, like Antibia in Anyte's poem, 'known for her beauty and cleverness', or like Eucharis the actress (second century A.D.): 'I was educated and taught as if by the Muses' hands. I adorned the nobility's festivals with my dancing, and first appeared before the common people in a Greek play.'[16] But then they had no husband or children to care for.

It is possible to claim that emphasis on chastity makes particular sense in a world whose contraceptive methodology was imperfect, and in which abortion was dangerous; as in the pseudo-Pythagorean treatise, 'The greatest glory a freeborn woman can have is the witness her own children will give to her chastity and toward her husband by bearing the stamp of likeness to the father whose seed produced them.'[17] Still, these problems don't appear to have affected everyone: think of Clodia or Messalina. One can also assume that to some degree some men 'projected' into women's psyches the more violent sex drive that in most societies appears to be characteristic of men. But these explanations may derive much of their conviction from the concerns of our own society. It might be simpler to conclude (particularly since we have inscriptions as evidence) that chastity and concern for the home were the qualities men valued most in their wives, and that they were hurt emotionally and financially by their wives' failure to perform these primary duties; cf. the first-century B.C. inscription for Aurelia Philematium, a freedwoman, by her husband Lucius, a butcher: 'My wife who died before me, my one and only, a loving woman who possessed my heart; she lived a faithful wife to a faithful husband with affection equal to my own, *since she never let avarice keep her from her duty*.'[18]

What women themselves thought about the value of their lives is more difficult to determine. Only a few documents survive that testify to the qualities of what Patricia Spacks calls 'the female

[15] '*Technikai kai Mousikai*: the education of women in the fourth century and in the Hellenistic period,' *AJAH* 2 (1977) 51-68.

[16] In *WLGR*.

[17] In *WLGR*.

[18] In *WLGR*.

imagination':[19] some poems of Sappho, a fragment of Erinna's *Distaff*; Sulpicia's elegies, the first person narrative of St. Perpetua of Carthage.[20] But these are documents written by highly educated women, with defined intellectual intentions. What would Clodia have said in her own defence? What would she have said about the actualities of her marriage with Quintus Metellus Celer, or about Catullus, or Caelius himself? Catullus at least records that he once loved her or someone like her, but his poetry, understandably, tells us not so much about her as what *he* feels about her; in his poetry she is the archetypal *puella*, his beloved, or, as in the *Pro Caelio*, the unfaithful, archetypal *meretrix*. The great advantage of their portrayals is that they are sufficiently general to have made Lesbia quite literally a classic, specific enough to be memorable, but general enough to have significance in any place or time.

But it is also important to remember that Cicero's portrait of Clodia is better literature than history, constructed with an ear for language and an understanding of comic technique, that relies for its best effects on insinuations and suggestions that would be inadmissible as evidence in a modern court of law. In the *Pro Cluentio* also, when Cicero describes how the citizens hid when Sassia passed through their towns, a judge today would demand times and names and places, but Cicero needed only to give his audience the suggestion of an analogue in epic, Medea in the third book of Apollonius, setting out in her wagon to find her lover Jason and so betray her home and family for sex and to begin a chain of murders that would end with the death of her own children.

I have tried to show that we will usually learn more from ancient documents about attitudes toward women than about what women themselves actually felt and did in ordinary circumstances, though sometimes, particularly in Greek drama, a character like Procne in Sophocles' *Tereus* will speak to the issues with which our few surviving women's voices are concerned.[21] But at the same time I think we would be mistaken not to see on the part of men great sympathy and respect for women's contribution to their lives, usually without sentiment or hypocrisy. We may regret as historians that the men define good and evil in women's character primarily in relation to themselves, but women, if they had more to say, might not have done it any better. The 'man who seems strong as the gods' in Sappho's poem is no more an individual than he is in Catullus' adaptation;[22] Perpetua in her narrative or her imprisonment

[19]Patricia Spacks, *The Female Imagination* (New York 1975).
[20]Above, pp.30-1.   [21]Above, p.20.
[22]Catullus 51; see below, p.65, n.12.

describes only what her father says to her and says to him. She does not try to account for his thoughts like a novelist. What matters to her is what she feels: 'But he left it at that and departed, vanquished along with his diabolical arguments. For a few days afterwards I gave thanks to the Lord that I was separated from my father, and I was comforted by his absence'(2.3-4). In this and subsequent encounters she answers his entreaties to her to return home with Christian cant. She is not any less insensitive in her treatment of him than the Hippocratic doctors were in their prescriptions for hysterical virgins; she too relies on what she has been taught and remains faithful to her colleagues. Her concern throughout is primarily with herself: 'My baby had got used to being nursed at the breast and to staying with me in prison. So I sent the deacon Pomponius away to my father to ask for the baby. But father refused to give him over. But as God willed, the baby had no further desire for the breast, nor did I suffer any inflammation; and so I was relieved of any anxiety for my child and of any discomfort in my breasts'(6.6). Men in her narrative are described only as punitive adversaries, like her father and the Roman governor, or as supportive friends, like her brother and the deacons. If women like Clodia had written poetry or orations, and we had knowledge of nothing else about Catullus, Caelius, or Cicero, I wonder what we would have thought of *them*?

5

Patterns of Women's Lives in Myth

The term 'myth' suggests to most people an entertaining tale, a scenario of an opera or ballet, which contains unpronounceable names and intriguingly Freudian plots. Incest, sibling rivalry and the like attract our attention, but otherwise it is hard to take the stories seriously.[1]

Yet in imperceptible ways classical mythology is still with us, at least in our literature. Whether we are aware of it or not, our perception of reality continues to be defined by the 'Greek experience'. My contention is simply that narrative patterns established in ancient times have shaped literary forms since antiquity. The plots of myths recur even in contemporary writing, with only names, dates and places changed.

Keeping to tradition has its advantages: it makes communication easy; it sells books. But it also limits understanding. Myths about women are a case in point. Take, for example, Jennifer Cavallieri in *Love Story*. Her type has been around since Orpheus' bride Eurydice: marry young (for love), die young and childless and lamented. Janice in *Rabbit, Run*, who drowns her baby, is a modern analogue of Medea, who killed her sons to spite her husband.

There are ancient prototypes for the heroines in most European literature. The trouble is that there are no myths about certain other

[1]The principal ancient sources for the myths cited in the text are as follows: The journey of the nine Muses: Hesiod *Theogony* 1-15. The birth of Aphrodite: ibid., 188-210, and *Homeric Hymn* 6. Artemis' journey: *Homeric Hymn* 27. The rape of Persephone: *Homeric Hymn* 2. Semele's violent death: Euripides *Bacchae*. Danae in the bronze-walled bedroom: Sophocles *Antigone* 944-5 and Simonides fr. 543. Io's journey: Aeschylus *Prometheus Bound*. Aphrodite and Anchises: *Homeric Hymn* 5. Clytemnestra: Aeschylus *Agamemnon*, esp. 11. Medea: Euripides *Medea*, esp 1242, 1245. Jocasta: Sophocles *Oedipus Tyrannus*. Agave and Pentheus: Euripides *Bacchae*. Athena: *Homeric Hymn* 28. Daphne: Ovid *Metamorphoses I* 452-567. Penelope: Homer *Odyssey*, esp. 2.121-2 (her mind). Phaedra: Euripides *Hippolytus*, esp. 406-7. Antigone: Sophocles *Antigone*, esp. 525. Emily Dickinson: 'Because I could not stop for Death,' no.712 (ed. Johnson).

types of female experience, for example, the successful married career woman or the woman who has children and remains an individual. This lack has a profound effect upon everyone who learns about life through literature, especially middle-aged college graduates, professors, and professionals – the very people who now are in a position to help women achieve equality.

Review the myths and you will discover that they offer women only three life patterns. The first is birth and rising to maturity. After this step woman in the myths has only two options: marriage and childbirth – resulting in her death (literal or figurative) as an individual – or withholding/destruction – resulting in the preservation of her individuality.

The first pattern, stated in outline form, seems reasonable enough. Men are also born, and they mature. But the process of development is characterised differently for each sex. The young man in the myths proves himself by skill, strength, or intelligence: he slays the dragon, he returns from death or captivity. The young woman travels, in the company of other maidens, singing and dancing, to the presence of some important male. We hear how the nine Muses are born and go up to meet their father Zeus in heaven; how Aphrodite, born in the sea foam, is dressed and brought to the company of the gods in heaven. Artemis, after the hunt each day, hangs up her bow and arrows and joins a group of dancing maidens in her brother Apollo's halls. The contemporary ritual analogue to these stories is the coming-out party: the maiden is dressed, trained in social conduct, and presented to society. The myth – and ritual – express the mysterious change of status that occurs at puberty. But while the males in myths attain maturity by self-assertion and creativity, the females remain passive: they join the dance; they are received into the established order.

The choice of females after coming out is even more restricted. If they choose to marry, they may either die themselves or kill their husbands and/or children. If they choose to remain celibate, they must do men's work or become frozen in some aspect of their maiden state; for example, they turn into trees. There are no other possibilities.

For convenience, we can examine each alternative separately.

The first possibility is marriage (or union), childbirth and death of the individual. This is the pattern behind the influential story of Persephone, who is stolen away by a husband who is literally death – Hades, Lord of the Dead. Consider Semele, the god Dionysus' mortal mother, who was destroyed by lightning when she asked to see her immortal lover Zeus in all his glory. The maiden Danae was sealed by her father in a bronze walled bedroom to keep her from contact with males, but the god Zeus rained in upon her in a shower of gold and she became pregnant. In consequence she was put out to sea with her infant son in a *larnax*, a storage chest or coffin. The maiden Io, who attracted the eye of Zeus, was changed into a cow and herded around the Mediterranean to Egypt, where she was delivered of a son, after which we hear nothing more about her. Life stops for these women with marriage (or sexual union) and/or childbirth. This concept of experience survives in the modern custom of a woman taking her husband's name at marriage and in the curious fact that birthday parties are given for the child rather than for his mother. Only the goddess Persephone can survive marriage as an individual because she is, in a sense, recycled: for half the year she leaves her husband and lives in heaven with her mother Demeter, becoming a maiden daughter once again.

The only way a married female can preserve her identity is to destroy the husband or children who have taken it away. This is the method used by Aphrodite, who abandons her consorts – like Aeneas' father Anchises, whom she leaves in bed shaken and fearful, announcing that she will return in five years with his son, who will be entrusted in the meantime to Nymphs (an ancient version of a day care centre). Clytemnestra is less considerate of her husband Agamemnon: she and her lover Aegisthus murder him in the bathtub. Then she sends her son Orestes into exile. Medea, abandoned by her husband Jason, gains mobility and individuality by murdering her two sons. Jocasta agrees to abandon her son Oedipus at birth and continues to reign as queen of Thebes until he returns and she discovers who he is. Agave, sister of the Semele who was annihilated by her lover Zeus, is memorable principally because she kills her son Pentheus in a Dionysiac frenzy, helps her sisters tear him to pieces, and returns home with his head speared on her ritual staff.

It is no wonder that some ancient women chose to avoid contact with men. Celibate females could at least perform men's creative work, for example, warfare (the goddess Athena's role) or hunting (the goddess Artemis' provenance). Or the celibate could be transformed, at the moment of decision, into a single characteristic of maidenhood. Daphne, for example, avoided Apollo's advances by becoming a laurel tree. Fixed in the ground, immobile, she avoided the journey or voyage that the impregnated Io or postpartum Danae was compelled to take and thus remained forever herself, *daphne* (which is Greek for laurel). Until recently at women's colleges Daphne's experience was commonly recreated in such rituals as the all-girl maypole dances at Bryn Mawr and the solemnly feminist Tree

Day at Wellesley (cf. below, ch.16).

It is tempting at this point to object. What about Penelope? What about the strong-minded, interesting women in Euripides' dramas? But closer investigation reveals that these women, too, conform to the patterns. Penelope is intelligent ('there is no mind like hers among Achaean women') but passive. She waits twenty years for her husband to return, taking in the meantime only withholding action: unweaving the shroud she is making for her father-in-law, postponing decisions. Her son Telemachus leaves on a dangerous trip and she is powerless to stop him. When her husband Odysseus returns disguised as a beggar, she does not seem completely aware of his identity. In her isolation, she compares herself to Procne, the nightingale who forever mourns the son she has murdered. In no respect does she seem able to take the initiative. The final contest for her hand among her suitors is set up by the goddess Athena. After Odysseus reveals his true identity (significantly, by indicating that he knows the secret construction of their marriage bed) and is reunited with her, we hear no more about her. She plays a role in the story only in her son's childhood and her husband's absence. When Telemachus proves himself a man and Odysseus returns, she disappears. Homer showed great insight in portraying simultaneously her unwillingness to lose autonomy and her desire to resume the conventional role of a Greek housewife.

Women in Euripides also protest their lot but, like Penelope, conform to it. Phaedra tries but cannot resist the passion that brings her death: 'I know well the deed, the disease, the dishonour, and I am well aware that I am also a woman, a hateful object to all.' Medea complains about the role of women – their restriction to the house, their subjugation by men, the pain of childbearing. But she offers no constructive solution to these problems. An alternative, such as making her own living as a witch doctor, does not come to mind. She (or Euripides) cannot conceive of a woman existing honourably or practically without male protection. Medea cannot easily kill her husband, so she destroys his weaker dependents – his new fiancée and prospective father-in-law – along with her own two sons and goes off to live in Athens with King Aegeus.

It is no coincidence that the dramas concern women who cannot accept what they are given: tragedy deals with human inability to come to terms with the irrational and uncontrollable. Antigone, in Sophocles' play, cannot accept the laws laid down by the king, her uncle Creon, and so she breaks them in the service of what she calls a higher morality. Still unmarried, she has the mobility and independence associated in other myths with 'creative maidens', like Artemis and Athena. But only the goddesses seem to be able to play quasi-masculine roles successfully. The mortal Antigone is sentenced to death both for her disobedience to Creon's law and for what would now be called role deviance. Her assertiveness disturbs king Creon: 'While I am alive no woman will rule me.' Aggressive feminine action in the dramas – whether Antigone's, Clytemnestra's, or Medea's – is characterised as masculine. Clytemnestra has 'a woman's heart that plans like a man's'. 'Put on heavy armour, my heart,' says Medea as she is about to kill her children; 'go toward the sad goal post of life.' The language is traditionally associated with the male occupations of war and athletics. In the unwritten laws of Athenian society, assertiveness and independence were exclusively male prerogatives.

Unfortunately, the narrative patterns of feminine existence did not perish with the society that produced them. To later antiquity the Greek experience was synonymous with civilisation. The works of Homer and the dramatists were required reading in all schools. Mythology thus survived in what might otherwise have been a hostile environment. For example, in the second century A.D. the cult of Isis provided opportunity to worship a female power far more comprehensive and constructive than any of the Greek goddesses. But Apuleius, a convert to the cult, wrote his allegory of Psyche, the soul, along standard narrative lines. The pregnant Psyche travels over the world in search of her husband Cupid, performing difficult tasks en route. But, unlike her male counterparts who undertake grand quests, she can accomplish nothing without assistance. She fails most conspicuously in her final mission, which is to bring a box unopened to Persephone. In curiosity she opens the box, falls into a deep sleep. and is rescued only by her husband. After her child is born, her story ends.

The recorded lives of the Christian saints reflect other traditional narrative patterns. St. Agnes was martyred just before a marriage that would have required renunciation of her faith. St. Barbara was confined in a tower and murdered by her father. St. Cecily was stifled and then bludgeoned to death in her bathroom. St. Theresa energetically founded new female orders. So the biographies of the bride of death, the inept female, and the creative maiden survived their Hellenic prototypes Io, Eurydice, Danae, and Artemis.

It would be convenient to blame this traditionalism on male chauvinism throughout the ages: after all, the myths put women in their place. But in fact the patterns also persist in literature composed by women. All Jane Austen's novels end with the marriage of the heroine. (Marriage is in fact the opening topic of *Pride and Prejudice*.)

Emily Dickinson writes of a carriage ride to the grave: she is wearing a thin gown and is accompanied by a courteous, gentlemanly Death. *Middlemarch* ends with the second and permanent marriage of its heroine. But George Eliot makes her own dissatisfaction with the traditional marriage-oblivion pattern explicit in the book's last pages:

> Certainly those determining acts of her life were not ideally beautiful. They were the mixed result of young and noble impulse, struggling amidst the conditions of an imperfect social state, in which great feelings will often take the aspect of error, and great faith the aspect of illusion . . . Her finely touched spirit had still its fine issues, though they were not widely visible. Her full nature, like that of the river of which Cyrus broke the strength, spent itself in channels which had no great name on the earth. But the effect of her being on those around her was incalculably diffusive: for the growing good of the world is partly dependent on unhistoric acts; and that things are not so ill with you or me as they might have been, is half owing to the number who live faithfully a hidden life, and rest in unvisited tombs.

The disparity between hope and actual achievement seems almost tragic. The heroine Dorothea, like a river, becomes in her socially imperfect marriage a non-individual, a series of nameless channels from which others draw strength. It seems impossible (at least in literature) for a woman to remain an entity without being an Artemis or a Medea.

Only in the twentieth century have women moved toward creating a new women's literature. In *To the Lighthouse* Virginia Woolf specifically illustrates how Mrs Ramsay is in fact the source of the life-giving channels that in Dorothea's case had gone unrecognised. In Sue Kaufman's *Diary of a Mad Housewife* the heroine embarks without assistance on a journey to self-discovery, and the journey ends in compromise with (not rescue by) her husband. Changing social conditions (like women's suffrage) helped make Virginia Woolf more aware of the importance and nature of woman's role than she might have been had she been born a generation earlier. The present women's movement has again made new awareness possible: we can see that most stories about women end too soon and that they needlessly restrict the range of possible accomplishment.

It is tantalising to speculate why the Greek patterns have persisted so long and in so many different contexts. Are narrative structures as durable as Indo-European grammar, which has maintained for three millennia that sentences ordinarily consist of subject, verb, and object and that action can be perceived in no other way? Or is it that the narrative patterns are true in terms of actual human experience?

That is, is it true that marriage guarantees death of the individual female, that a woman is free only if she is celibate, divorced, or childless? Does myth influence experience or experience influence myth? The answer is, of course, that they act upon each other and that the interaction is subconscious and gradual.

The Greek view of female experience thus lingers on, even though medicine and industrial technology make other life styles available. It would be foolish to expect a rapid change. Many more people, after all, read and saw *Love Story* than *Diary of a Mad Housewife*. Tradition is comfortable; we can place ourselves in it, as in a favourite chair. But it is useful sometimes to look at traditions (and our old furniture) critically. Feminine experience in the eighth century B.C. had, along with its pastoral charms, severe intellectual and emotional limitations. To see life in the twentieth century in these terms is amusing and convenient, but it denies us the chance to know and be ourselves.

6

Women's Rights

The women who occupy the centre stage so often determine the outcome of Greek dramas that it is easy to forget that none of them commits any act without a man's help. Clytemnestra has Aegisthus, Medea finds asylum with Aegeus before she kills the princess and her children. Hecuba gets Agamemnon's consent before she takes revenge on her son's murderer, Polymestor. But to an Athenian audience such dependency would not seem remarkable. Athenian women had title only to their jewellery and the clothes on their backs; everything else, their marriage, their property, their dowry, remained under the control of male relatives.

David Schaps's book[1] painstakingly describes the legal institutions that determined women's economic status. Laws kept the inherited property of a woman without brothers under the control of her father's family, not her husband's; a woman's guardian (or *kyrios*) had power to transact all business for her; a husband could dispose of his wife's dowry, even though the dowry was always spoken of as *hers*; women were involved in petty, but never lucrative, trades. It appears that women outside Athens had somewhat more control over their lives and property. For example, the law code of Gortyn in Crete allowed a woman to pick her own husband if no men in her own family or clan were available or wanted her. But no evidence exists to show how often a woman in fact was able to exercise this vestigial right. Only in Hellenistic times, and then at first outside Greece, did women begin to have primary control over their inheritance and property.

To assemble all the evidence bearing on these problems is an extraordinary service. Relevant information lies scattered in inscriptions not previously classified, in lawyers' arguments that present only one side of a case, in situations of fourth-century comedy. Schaps takes into consideration the varying nature of his source material; he never sidesteps problems of conflicting evidence; he never tries to resolve an issue where data seem incomplete. His

[1] David M. Schaps, *Economic Rights of Women in Ancient Greece* (Edinburgh 1979).

dispassionate, reasoned approach is particularly welcome in a field of inquiry where hostilities are easily aroused. Lively translations and non-technical language make the book accessible to those who know neither law nor Greek. But nonetheless the book will appeal more to professionals because Schaps has so closely limited his scope, and does not attempt to re-examine more familiar works of literature and historical events in the light of his findings.

Yet indications are that economic factors alone did not bring about the improvement in women's status that marks the Hellenistic age. Could money alone have brought independence, women would have become property owners soon after coinage was invented, when they no longer needed to rely on men to manage and defend the family land. A prostitute like the infamous Neaera could buy her freedom by taking up a collection from former lovers, and with her significant earnings maintain a sizeable household staff, yet throughout her life like every other woman in Athens she was dependent on a man or men. One suspects that the practices of less restrictive societies eventually had some influence; that among the upper classes at least, literacy and improved medical practice played some role. Economic rights, as Schaps suggests throughout his books, are bound up with social attitudes; no study of women's rights can be complete without consideration of how and why women came to be regarded as mentally, emotionally, and morally capable of performing financial transactions and of managing property.

7

Girls' Choruses

So scattered through the literature are references to girls' choruses that it has been hard to see among them similarities that in fact exist. Calame's Vol. I,[1] a comprehensive study of the function of these choruses, performs the valuable service of bringing citations together and of arranging them in context, so that significant patterns emerge. His findings improve understanding of many customs and allusions. Some examples: since a chorus regularly is composed of persons of the same age (pp.66ff.), Pi. *Isthm.* 8.1, *Kleandrōi halikiai te* will refer to the group chosen to celebrate the victory (cf. Köhnken, *BICS* 22, 1975, 25-6); since in Bacchyl. 11.82ff. the Proetids' madness concerns the transition from maiden-hood, marked also in rites of passage like the Brauronia, the celebration to commemorate the myth involves choruses of girls (pp.417ff.); since in the songs gracelessness regularly denotes girlhood, and beauty the moment of transition to womanhood, Sappho's line about Atthis, *smikra pais k'acharis* (49 LP) describes the prepubescent phase when homoerotic relations were considered normal (pp.400-1) – other cases in point would be Erinna's *Distaff* (see now S. Pomeroy *ZPE* 32, 1978, 17-22 and the races run by nude girls to Artemis at Brauron (evidence in Kahil, cited by Calame p.187 n.29) and to Athena at Argos (Callim., *Lav. Pal.* 23-9; cf. Theoc. 18.21-4, Calame p.339).

Particularly interesting for the study of women in the ancient world is Calame's discussion of the female chorus as *paideia*, which explains the social function of women's love for one another, and the older woman's role as teacher. In this larger context a third-century commentator's description of Sappho *paideuousa tas aristas* (*SLG* S 261.7-11) can hardly be taken as support for the old notion of Sappho's 'school' (see now also K. J. Dover, *Greek Homosexuality*, London 1978, 175). Calame observes that terminology of domestic animals clearly marks the girls' chorus as separate from the dominant

[1]Claude Calame, *Les Choeurs de jeunes filles en Grèce archaïque. I. Morphologie, fonction religieuse et sociale. II. Alcman.* Filologia e Critica. Istituto di filologia classica. Università di Urbino. Vols. 20,21. Rome, 1977.

male system (pp.411ff.). But he does not comment in his otherwise exhaustive 'morphology' of the chorus on another important distinguishing feature of women's ritual. All choruses describe themselves, since it is essential for them to establish their particular corporate identity (Lefkowitz, *HSCP* 67, 1963, 195; S. C. Humphreys, *Anthropology and the Greeks*, London 1978, 219). But since girls' choruses concentrate far more than men's on physical appearance and sexuality, they give a relative impression of greater ephemerality and triviality, at least when judged by the values of the male world. Calame's second volume uses the findings of the first as a background for detailed discussion of Alcman, frr. 1 and 3. By proceeding from general pattern to particular instance Calame endows these elusive and fragmentary poems with a coherence they seem previously to have lacked. Homosexual allusions in fr. 1 have a primarily paideutic function. The chorus leader Hagesichora is accompanied by her *erōmenē* Agido. Aenesimbrota, in whose house one finds the chorus members (73), is a teacher-trainer like Sappho. The two leaders 'fight' (60ff.) not against a rival chorus, but in order to enact their ritual role on behalf of the whole group in a ceremony that marks the transition from girlhood to womanhood; calling these two girls 'doves' suggests a vulnerable femininity. Comparisons of the leaders to winning race-horses and to a trace-horse again suggest the discipline of their future roles. Constant references to the girls' faces and hair also call attention to their marriageability. Initial mention of the Dioscuri and the Hippocoontidae marks the song as a peculiarly Lacedaemonian ritual; terms like 'cousin' (52) and the name Astymelousa (3.64) are particularly suited to the close-knit Spartan community. Agido may even be a royal name. Helen herself, as goddess of the morning (Orthria, 62) presides over the ceremony in fr. 1, in which Agido 'bears witness' (cf. Pind., fr. 94b. 39) to Hagesichora, and the girls participate in a footrace, as in Theoc. 18.22 (cf. also Callim., *Lav. Pal.* 23-9). Calame's reconstruction will appeal to students both of archaic lyric and of women's role. Anyone familiar with the complex scholarship on these poems will be grateful for his clear charting of previous interpretations, his complete bibliography, and his detailed notes and indices.

But one wonders whether Calame's logical and lucid exposition has not been achieved at the cost of putting himself at some distance from the text. His structuralist methodology borrows from linguistics an interest in discovering relationships between separate words and discrete phenomena; it is not well suited to describing variations in content or in style. Calame speaks of the myths of youthful heroes involved in 'sexual combat' (p.56) where the chorus merely mentions names. He does not comment on why the tone of the *parthenia* seems remarkably informal: there are frequent questions and answers, direct comments on personal appearance; phrasing tends to be unadorned, e.g. in the moral to the myth, 'there is such a thing as gods' vengeance' (1.36), or in the prayer, 'receive their . . . , gods; from gods [comes] accomplishment and an end' (*ana kai telos*, 82-3). One might also note that in Alcman the chorus's praise for their leaders shows no trace of the *phthonos* that ordinarily accompanies a *man's* success (e.g., Pind., *Pyth.* 8.84-7). Apparently in *parthenia* excellence can be tolerated, because leadership among maiden groups is accorded not by competition but by birth (as for Nausicaa, *Od.* 6.109). The girls work together in harmony; homoerotic relations cause no tension; the emphasis falls on looks, not on emotion, as in Sappho or Erinna. In the *parthenia* the chorus's lives are as untroubled as their diction is uncomplicated. Epitaphs from later periods also testify to the continuing importance of close friendships among women and of one's *hēlikia* (e.g., Kaibel 73,78). But the *parthenia* provide the most immediate documentation of how the ancient public wished to think young girls behaved.

8

The Motivations
for St. Perpetua's Martyrdom

Let me summarise briefly how and what we know about the story of St. Perpetua's martyrdom. A narrator tells us about a group of Christians who were executed in Carthage in 203, including Vibia Perpetua, 'a newly married woman of good family and upbringing . . . about twenty-two years old . . . with an infant son at the breast'; with her is her brother, also a Christian convert (2.1-2). The narrator then quotes directly from Perpetua's own memoirs, which consist of her account of her imprisonment and of the dreams she had in prison; she tells how her father, who has remained a pagan, pleads with her to abandon her religion and tries to get the authorities to let her out; detailed, explicit visions tell her meanwhile that she must die. The narrator then tells the story of her fellow martyrs and their joint execution: they were exposed to wild beasts in the arena; Perpetua herself was attacked, but not seriously wounded, by a wild cow and finally killed by a gladiator, whose sword she willingly guided to her neck.

As you can tell even from this summary, there is ample subject matter here for many sermons, as Bishop Augustine of Hippo knew.[1] The *Acts of SS. Perpetua and Felicity* is, of course, a document that is meant to convert and persuade, and as such should be considered no more directly historical or objective than Angela Davis's autobiography.[2] But the story even so can tell us much about the working beliefs of the early church and in particular about the experience of a female martyr. In this chapter I would like to suggest,

[1]Augustine *Sermons* 280-2 (P.L. 38.1280-6); Tertullian *de An.*55.4 cites Perpetua's testimony as evidence for the privileged position of martyrs in heaven. All citations from Acts of the Christian martyrs are from Herbert Musurillo's text (Oxford 1972).
[2]On the historicity of the text, see H. Delehaye, *Les Passions des martyrs et les genres littéraires* (Brussels 1921), 63-73; R. Aigrain, *L'Hagiographie* (Poitiers 1953) 203; and esp. E. R. Dodds, *Pagan and Christian in an Age of Anxiety* (Cambridge 1965), 47-53, who suggests that unconventional elements in the narrative, such as Perpetua's dreams, are indications of its authenticity.

on the basis of her autobiographical account, that part of the appeal of the new religion lay in its encouragement to the convert to break traditional family patterns, and in its promise of enabling the convert to share in a new existence in a more egalitarian community.

In her dreams and in her life, Perpetua gives up her old family for a new one of brothers and sisters in Christ: she refuses to give in to her father, who visits her twice in prison, and finally throws himself at her feet in despair; she never mentions her brother or her mother after she sees in her dream that she must die, and she allows her father to take her nursing baby from her. We can recognise in Perpetua's resistance to her father and gradual withdrawal from her family the standard behaviour pattern of conversion; a wish to break with the past, a need to substitute strong new ties that can replace the old. The martyrs Agape, Irene and Chione of Salonica (we are told) 'abandoned their native city, their family, their property, and possessions because of love of God, and their expectation of heavenly things', and to avoid their persecutors went for two consecutive years (303 and 304) to live with each other on a mountain. One thinks of Lucius in Apuleius' *Metamorphoses*, who after his dream of Isis and transformation back into human shape, does not go home again, but joins a priesthood that serves and respects the feminine power he once tried to control and to exploit. Jerome advises Heliodorus, who wants to become a monk, to trample his father underfoot if his father lies down on the doorstep to block his passage (*per calcatum perge patrem, Ep.* 14.2). So Perpetua's father throws himself at her feet (5.5), and she dreams of treading on a snake to climb a ladder to heaven (4.6–11) and of stepping on the head of an Egyptian who opposes her in single combat (8.7). The metaphor in Jerome's advice and in Perpetua's dreams is the same, but it is noteworthy that in Perpetua's case the aggressive child is a woman.

There is a distinctive emphasis in stories of Christian women's martyrdom on separation from the family and on death as a means to life. Pagan women martyrs were celebrated by their contemporaries for their defiance of tyranny and loyalty to their husbands, and courage in the face of death.[3] One thinks especially of Arria, thrusting the sword into her breast, and saying to her husband in encouragement, 'Paetus, it doesn't hurt' (Pliny, *Ep.* 3.16.3). Arria's immortality, like Octavia's, consists only of being assured of continued fame, through celebration of her achievement in literature, Pliny's *Letters*, Tacitus' *Annals*. The Christians Perpetua, Agape, Irene and Chione die courageously but in noticeable isolation from

---

[3] Fannius (Pliny, 5.5) and Titinius Capito (8.12) wrote martyrologies; cf. the increasing concentration on death scenes in Tacitus' account of the reign of Nero.

their families, in defiance of, rather than in loyalty to, their husbands or fathers.[4] We find in the stories of the Christian women martyrs a surprising eagerness to abandon young infants: Perpetua, who at first is concerned for her nursing baby (3.6-7) and is relieved to get permission to keep him, after her dream about the snake and the ladder and a confrontation with her father, is miraculously relieved of her responsibility, 'and as God willed, the baby wanted no more of the breast, nor did they (her breasts) give me fever, so that I was not tormented by care for the baby or the pain in my breasts' (6.8). Felicity, the slave girl who is imprisoned along with her, prays that she may be delivered of her child in time to be executed along with the others, and rejoices when she does in fact give birth to a little girl prematurely (15.1-2). Similarly, Eutychia, one of the women tried in Salonica along with Irene, though seven months pregnant, insists, in spite of danger of imprisonment and death, to keep the faith (3). To celibate male scholars this behaviour may appear less remarkable (or perhaps more commendable) than it does to us. It might more accurately be viewed as an abnormal, extreme form of social protest: we can compare the accounts in Greek myth of groups of Theban women who fled to the mountains to worship a new god, abandoning their homes and children, and in some cases even murdering their sons. Euripides in the *Bacchae* portrays Agave's condition as a kind of temporary insanity; modern anthropologists would compare it to the sudden ecstatic experiences that bring oppressed groups a sense (albeit transient) of political power.[5] Were the Christian women who fled their families by rushing to the wilderness, or to prison, abandoning their babies, also seeking a new freedom from the traditional patterns of their lives?

That the nature of these women's conduct was regarded as something more than simple impiety is indicated by the nature of their punishment: Irene, because she had concealed forbidden written material before she 'ran away' into the wilderness, is sentenced to be placed naked in the brothel, on a subsistence diet (5). The judge Aquila in Alexandria (*c* 210) threatens to let his gladiators rape the Christian Potamiaena, but then has her executed by having boiling pitch poured drop by drop over different parts of her body (3). As in the case of the woman who murdered her husband, child and husband's sister in Apuleius and is condemned to be mounted by the jackass in

[4]Cf. also the story of the slave Sabina, who was bound and cast out on the mountains by her mistress and rescued by fellow Christians (Pionius, 9.4); and the isolation of a Christian woman accused of adultery but ultimately rescued by other Christians (Jerome, *Ep.* 1); explicit bodily torture and savage male accusers are standard elements in these stories.

[5]See I. M. Lewis, *Ecstatic Religion* (Baltimore, 1971) 30-2, 66-99.

the arena, male superiority must be publicly reasserted in case of female attack on familial or governmental norms – as Creon says to Antigone, 'while I'm alive no woman will rule me' (525).[6] In Perpetua's case, where the principal antagonist is not a Roman governor, but rather her own father, there are also sexual overtones. Her dreams reveal a concern with destroying threatening male figures: she treads upon a snake (4.6) and in her final vision becomes a man in order to step on the head of an Egyptian (8.11-14). The explanation of the repeated metaphor of trampling becomes apparent when we remember that her father, in their last interview, threw himself at her feet (5.5). In her dreams there is a curiously consistent association of feet with power: she describes how the Egyptian 'tried to get hold of my feet, but I kept striking him on the face with the heels of my feet' (10.1). In her descriptions of the kind deacon who leads her to victory, and of the trainer who presides over her successful contest, she calls attention to their sandals, 'elaborate' (10.1) and 'complex, made from gold and silver' (10.7). Her desire to compete in these dream-contests successfully against her father indicates that, in her perception at least, more than theological issues are involved in her martyrdom. As Marie-Louise von Franz has shown in her Jungian analysis, Perpetua's death is in part a result of an adolescent rejection necessary for personal individuation.[7] But the consistent emphasis in the narrative on sexual definition suggests a more specific motivation, what psychotherapists call 'unconscious incest', a close emotional pairing of father and daughter, which results from a desperate attempt to keep a disintegrating family together.[8] You will recall that while the narrator of Perpetua's story says that she was honourably married, her husband is never mentioned by name, and appears nowhere in the narrative. Because she appears to be in her father's custody, we might assume that she is widowed or divorced. More noteworthy than the absence of her husband is the shadowy role played by her mother in the story (she seems to be imprisoned with Perpetua at the beginning, and Perpetua turns the child over to her care, 3.7; the father begs Perpetua to think of her mother; thereafter the mother disappears from the narrative). Perpetua's main concern throughout is with her father ('for a few days I gave thanks to the Lord that I was separated from my father, and was comforted by his absence', 3.4); she feels pity for him, she tries to console him (5.5-6, 9.3). She records first

[6]Cf. also Creon's admonition re Antigone and Ismene: 'From now on they must be women and not let loose (i.e., out-of-doors)' (578-9, with Jebb's note).

[7]M.-L. von Franz, 'Die Passio Perpetuae' in C. J. Jung, Aion (Zurich 1951), 389-495.

[8]See R. D. Laing, Politics of the Family (London 1972), 12-15.

his rage ('he moved toward me as though he would pluck my eyes out', 3.3), then his sorrow ('pity me . . . if I am worthy to be called your father, if I have favoured you above all your brothers', 5.2; 'with tears in his eyes he no longer addressed me as daughter, but as woman', *non filiam sed dominam*, 5.5). But her reply to his plea is remote, 'it will all happen . . . as God wills' (5.6), and she accepts death eagerly, as the narrator observes, 'she screamed as she was struck on the bone, then took the trembling hand of the young gladiator and guided it to her throat. It was as though so great a woman, feared as she was by the unclean spirit could not be dispatched unless she herself were willing' (21.9-10).[9] Similar patterns of actions and reactions are found in unconscious (and conscious) incestuous father-daughter relationships; the absent husband and the absent mother, and, to replace her, the close emotional pairing of the daughter with the father, and the daughter's eventual withdrawal and self-destructive behaviour – for example the case of Ilse, who put her hand in the burning stove and said to her father, 'Look, this is to show how much I love you.'[10] St. Dymphna, according to the legend, after her father lost his wife and decided to take his daughter as her successor, fled from Ireland to Belgium, where she founded (not inappropriately) a mental hospital; in the French tale of the donkey-skin, again it is the daughter who must find an escape and atone for her predicament by disfiguring herself.[11] In patriarchal society, ancient and modern, the guilt for an incestuous relationship is (remarkably) felt only by the younger, passive partner: self-destruction or self-negation in some form results, suicidal depression, inability to have a mature sexual relationship with another man.[12]

It is not without significance that the religion which Perpetua

[9] Cf. the scene in Euripides' *Hecabe*, where Polyxena bares her breast to receive her executioner's sword in an ambivalent desire to avoid becoming a slave-concubine (557-70), and the emphasis on sexuality in Prudentius' description of the death of St. Agnes, *Peristephanon* 14.74-8.

[10] L. Binswanger, 'Insanity as life-historical phenomenon and as mental disease: the case of Ilse' (orig. publ. 1945), in *Existence* (New York 1963).

[11] On St. Dymphna, the tale of the donkey-skin, and similar stories, see H. Günter, *Psychologie der Legende: Studien zu einer wissenschaftlichen Heiligen-Geschichte* (Freiburg 1949), 54-6. Note also that it is Myrrha, not Cinyras, who is blamed in the story and who undergoes metamorphosis (Ovid, *Met.*, 10.298-502).

[12] See Lustig, et al, 'Incest: a family group survival pattern', in *Discussion, Adult Seduction of the Child, Medical Aspects of Human Sexuality* (March, 1973); confirmed in clinical practice of J. Fineman and S. M. Havens. See now also J. Herman and L. Hirschman, 'Father-daughter incest,' *Signs* 2.4 (1977) 737-9. The pattern of defensive 'incest' here described does not appear to be related to the brother-sister incest of which Christians were regularly accused by pagans; see M. Smith, *Clement of Alexandria and a Secret Gospel of Mark* (Cambridge, Mass., 1973) 234.

adopts appears to encourage more a-sexual, fraternal relationships between men and women, and that the men with whom she dies and whom she sees in her visions are benign, supportive, and beautiful, as opposed to the hostile (her father wants to tear out her eyes, 3.3) and mutilated (her father tears out his beard, 9.2; she sees in a dream her young brother who had died of skin ulcers, 7.5). Her willingness to die is not only an act of faith and maturity, but in existential terms, a political act against her environment. In seeking martyrdom she was as much concerned with solving problems in this life as with attaining perfection in the next. The Church Fathers, as Bishop Augustine's sermons indicate, would emphasise in this document the importance of what E. M. Forster called, in a bitter story, 'The Life to Come', and they would praise Perpetua and Felicity for acting uncharacteristically for women, in overcoming the inherent weakness and sinfulness of their flesh.[13] We may regret that these men did not also wish to realise how Christianity in its earlier stages also met a social need of releasing women from the hierarchical structure imposed by patriarchal society, which the church in its own organisation would increasingly incorporate and emulate. The persistent emphasis on breaking with family and on sexually defined conflict with authority in the *Acts* of Perpetua, Irene and Potamiaena express a perceived concern of women in the early centuries of the Christian era.

[13]See esp. Augustine *Serm.* 280.5, 281.1, 282.3. On the consistent failure of male scholars to acknowledge the positive significance of femininity in the performance of certain heroic acts, see D. Daube, *Civil Disobedience in Antiquity* (Edinburgh, 1972) 5-6. See also R. Ruether, 'Misogynism and virginal feminism in the Early Church', in *Religion and Sexism* (New York, 1974) 150-83.

9

Critical Stereotypes
and the Poetry of Sappho

Criticism of creative art seems curiously dependent on biography.[1] It appears difficult to separate an artist's life from his work, or to regard literature or music or paintings primarily as public statements. Since the act of creation is assumed fundamentally to be an emotional response, the artist is viewed as an active participant in the world he has created. In the case of male writers, the assumption seems always to be that the artist, whether Catullus, Brahms or Goya, uses the full range of his intellectual powers to come to terms with his problems. It is understood that the methods and the problems vary considerably from artist to artist. But in the case of female artists, the assumptions on which criticism is based tend to be more narrowly defined: (1) *Any creative woman is a 'deviant', that is, women who have a satisfactory emotional life (home, family and husband) do not need additional creative outlets.* The assumption behind this assumption is that 'deviance' in the case of women results from being deprived of men – in other words, women artists tend to be *(a)* old maids or *(b)* lesbians, either overt female homosexuals or somehow 'masculine'. (2) *Because women poets are emotionally disturbed, their poems are psychological outpourings, i.e. not intellectual but ingenuous, artless, concerned with their inner emotional lives.* As a result, criticism of two such different poets as Sappho and Emily Dickinson can sound remarkably alike.

Dr John Cody's recent analysis of Emily Dickinson's poem 'I had been hungry all the Years' provides a vivid illustration of the special criticism applied to female artists. I prefer to begin with Emily Dickinson rather than with Sappho, because Dickinson wrote in English (which I understand better than I do Greek), and because the facts of her life are relatively well documented: she was a recluse, unmarried, wore white, wrote in the bedroom of her house in Amherst

[1] See esp. Harold F. Cherniss, 'The biographical fashion in literary criticism', *CPCP* 12.15 (1943) 279–92.

poems on little pieces of paper, some of which were published in her lifetime.

> I had been hungry, all the Years –
> My Noon had Come – to dine –
> I trembling drew the Table near –
> And touched the Curious Wine –
>
> 'Twas this on Tables I had seen –
> When turning, hungry, Home
> I looked in Windows, for the Wealth
> I could not hope – for Mine –
>
> I did not know the ample Bread –
> 'Twas so unlike the Crumb
> The Birds and I had often shared
> In Nature's – Dining Room –
>
> The Plenty hurt me – 'twas so new –
> Myself felt ill – and odd –
> As Berry – of a Mountain Bush –
> Transplanted – to the Road –
>
> Nor was I hungry – so I found
> That Hunger – was a way
> Of Persons outside Windows –
> The Entering – takes away –

(579 Johnson, *c* 1862)

My own impression of this poem is that its primary concern is disappointment: something long-awaited comes; once you have it, it disappears; thus in retrospect the anticipation seems more rewarding than the thing itself. The central thought is expressed in the terminology of food: the narrator of the poem is 'hungry'; then 'noon' (the dinner hour) has come like a guest, to dinner; there is a table with 'Curious Wine' (the narrator doesn't know what it is). The narrator had been like the birds, eating what was left; now he/she leaves the wilds, and his/her exclusion . . . and enters the house. The hunger then goes away and there is nothing. The bread and wine in the poem may take on additional significance if we think of them as elements in the Christian sacrament of the Eucharist: Dickinson was raised by devout church-goers, and drew much of her subject matter and metrical structure from the hymns she heard as a child.[2] Then the poem might also say: after receiving Communion, what does one have?

To our impressions we can compare what Dr Cody says in *After Great Pain: The Inner Life of Emily Dickinson.* He reads the poem as an

[2]On Dickinson's use of hymn metres and form see Thomas H. Johnson, *Emily Dickinson: An Interpretive Biography* (Cambridge, Mass. 1955) 84–6.

analyst would interpret dreams, along canonical Freudian lines: hunger connotes sexual experience, and Emily Dickinson's[3]

> imbibing of physical affection quickly becomes a glut and overwhelms her painfully. The experience is novel in an uncongenial way and causes her to sicken and feel strange. She feels that sexuality is too common a territory for her (a 'Road') because she is acclimated to an unfrequented and lofty habitat. (She comes of a 'Mountain Bush' and feels out of place, perhaps degraded, in the 'Road'; one senses in this word unpleasant connotations of too easy accessibility, prosaic purposes, dustiness, and commercial transactions.)

Once we accept the premise that the poem primarily concerns sex, it is possible to interpret its imagery more specifically:

> It is a commonplace that a woman's introduction to sexual intimacies may be frightening and disappointing. The bruising of delicate membranes may draw blood. Thus, the line 'The Plenty hurt me – 'twas so new' may refer not only to the overpowering emotion generated by her own and another's passion but also to the overwhelming and painful effects of physical force. The transplanted berry may be the hymeneal blood (the first colour commonly associated with berries is red); the Mountain Bush', the mons veneris; and the 'Road', the vagina. We cannot imagine that Emily Dickinson was unaware of these anatomical facts.

Whether or not she was more than 'dimly aware' of these 'unconscious sexual preoccupations' is not the issue: Cody's analysis enables us to see that Emily Dickinson, who 'has for so long been thought of as an ethereal other-world creature' was in fact 'a living flesh-and-blood woman who, Victorian Age notwithstanding, was well aware that whether she liked it or not she had no choice but to share in the physiological reactions of the rest of humanity'.[4]

If we in turn analyse Dr Cody's analysis, we find that it rests on several questionable assumptions: (1) That poems are like dreams, that is, are individual expressions of emotional problems, rather than public statements meant to be understood by and communicated to a large audience who had not read Freud on roads, berries, etc. But Emily Dickinson, as her correspondence shows, was most interested in getting into print and being recognised. (2) That Dickinson's problem is sexual deprivation, specifically, inability to accept or to enjoy men, an interpretation read in from her biography.

The same basic assumptions tend to be made about Sappho's famous fr. 31, though in less vividly stated forms. Compared with Emily Dickinson's, we know virtually nothing about Sappho's life. We can glean from biographies and passing references written long

[3]John Cody, *After Great Pain: The Inner Life of Emily Dickinson* (Cambridge, Mass. 1971) 141. [4]Ibid. 142.

after her death the names of her family, that she lived in Mytilene at the end of the seventh century, that she wrote nine books of lyric poetry, that she was a female homosexual, short, dark and ugly, and that she died by throwing herself off the White Rock in West Greece because of her unrequited love for a ferryman named Phaon ('shining'). Much of this information seems to have been derived from interpretations by ancient scholars (all male) of her poetry, some also from caricatures of her in comedy; the story of her death is obviously based on myth.[5] Again a portrait emerges of an emotional deviant: deprived because of her ugliness of male attention (like the ferryman's) which she craves.

Thus biography, itself derived from interpretation of the poems, is in turn reapplied to the poems and affects our interpretation of them. In the case of fr. 31 especially, much influential criticism has tended to centre on the 'facts' of Sappho's life:

> φαίνεταί μοι κῆνος ἴσος θέοισιν
> ἔμμεν' ὤνηρ, ὄττις ἐνάντιός τοι
> ἰσδάνει καὶ πλάσιον ἆδυ φωνεί-
> σας ὑπακούει
>
> καὶ γελαίσας ἰμέροεν, τό μ' ἦ μὰν
> καρδίαν ἐν στήθεσιν ἐπτόαισεν·
> ὠς γὰρ ἔς σ' ἴδω βρόχε', ὤς με φώναι-
> σ' οὐδ' ἒν ἔτ' εἴκει,
>
> ἀλλ' ἄκαν μὲν γλῶσσα †ἔαγε†, λέπτον
> δ' αὔτικα χρῶι πῦρ ὑπαδεδρόμηκεν,
> ὀππάτεσσι δ' οὐδ' ἒν ὄρημμ', ἐπιρρόμ-
> βεισι δ' ἄκουαι,
>
> †ἔκαδε μ' ἴδρως ψῦχρος κακχέεται†, τρόμος δὲ
> παῖσαν ἄγρει, χλωροτέρα δὲ ποίας
>
> ἔμμι, τεθνάκην δ' ὀλίγω 'πιδεύης
> φαίνομ' ἔμ' αὔται·
>
> ἀλλὰ πὰν τόλματον ἐπεὶ †καὶ πένητα†

The man seems to me strong as a god, the man who sits across from you and listens to your sweet talk nearby

and your lovely laughter – which, when I hear it, strikes fear in the heart in my breast. For whenever I glance at you, it seems that I can say nothing at all

[5]On the evidence for Sappho's life see especially Thomas McEvilley, 'Imagination and reality in Sappho' (diss. Univ. Cincinnati, 1968; University Microfilms nos 68-15, 166) 259-63. On the significance of the myth of Sappho's death, see Gregory Nagy, 'Phaethon, Sappho's Phaon, and the White Rock of Leukas', HSCP 77 (1973) 141-3, 172-7.

but my tongue is broken in silence, and that instant a light fire rushes beneath my skin, I can no longer see anything in my eyes and my ears are thundering,

and cold sweat catches hold of me, and shuddering hunts me all over, and I am greener than grass, and I seem to myself to be little short of death

But all is endurable, since even a poor man . . .

Wilamowitz saw 'that man' in the poem's first stanza as the husband of the girl. The girl is one of Sappho's students, and the poem concerns the man and schoolmistress Sappho's jealousy of him.[6] This interpretation transposes the poem to the realm of sexual normality: there is no evidence at all in the text that 'that man' is a husband, or the girl Sappho's pupil, or that Sappho ran a girl's school.[7] Page, in what is recognised as the authoritative English commentary on Sappho, is aware of the limitations of Wilamowitz' criticism, but still retains the same basic assumptions about the poem. In his analysis, he realises that the man only appears in the first stanza, but at the same time he is reluctant to take his attention off him:[8]

> But we must not forget that the *man* was the principal subject of the whole first stanza; and we shall not be content with any explanation of the poem which gives no satisfactory account of his presence and his prominence in it. If Sappho wishes to describe nothing more than the symptoms of her passion for the girl, what motive could she have for connecting that description thus closely with an occasion when the girl is engaged in merry conversation with a man? Surely that occasion is not devoid of all significance: and then it appears impossible to exclude the element of jealousy from Sappho's emotional response to the scene. Sappho loves the girl: and it is clearly suggested that the girl is not, at least at this moment, particularly interested in Sappho. Sappho is present in the company: but it is the man, not Sappho, who is sitting close by the girl, rejoicing in her laughter and converse. To maintain that Sappho feels no jealousy of the man would be to ignore the certain response of human nature to a situation of the type described, and to deprive the introduction of the man, and his relation to the girl, of all significance. On this point, at least, there is little room for doubt.

[6]Ulrich von Wilamowitz-Moellendorff, *Sappho und Simonides* (Berlin 1913) 58. Wilamowitz, in his interpretation, was attempting to restore objectivity to the criticism of Sappho's poetry: 'When the name Sappho is mentioned today, more people will think of sexual perversion than of a great poetess' (p.17). On the question of Sappho's sexual preference(s), see now esp. K. J. Dover, *Greek Homosexuality* (London 1978) 171-84.

[7]The authority of Wilamowitz continues to make scholars uneasy about abandoning the girls' school hypothesis; see, for example, R. Merkelbach, 'Sappho und ihr Kreis', *Philologus* 101 (1957) 1-29. Two recent school texts treat it as a live possibility: David A. Campbell, *Greek Lyric Poetry* (New York 1967) 261, and Douglas E. Gerber, *Euterpe* (Amsterdam 1970) 161; see my review of Campbell, *AJP* 91 (1970) 467-8.

[8]D. L. Page, *Sappho and Alcaeus* (Oxford 1955) 28.

The girl is talking to him, and not to Sappho; the physical symptoms that Sappho describes in such detail result specifically from jealousy. In addition, Page tends to see the poem as a direct outpouring of emotion, in much the same way that Dr Cody read Dickinson. Sappho's language[9]

> is realistic, severely plain and candid, unadorned by literary artifice. First, very quietly, 'I have no longer any power to speak'. Then she says something – we do not know exactly what – about her tongue. Then in simple words, 'a subtle fire has stolen beneath my flesh', and still more simply 'with my eyes I see nothing'. Then a homely metaphor, 'my ears are humming': and the next phrase could not be more bleak and un-adorned, whether the words meant 'sweat pours down me' or 'a cold sweat covers me'. Then, without artifice, 'a trembling seizes me all over'; thereafter an image which owes nothing to literary tradition, and surely reflects her own manner of thought and speech, 'paler than grass am I'; and finally the homeliest phrase of all, 'I seem to fall a little short of being dead'. Rarely, if anywhere, in archaic or classical poetry shall we find language so far independent of literary tradition, apparently so close to the speech of every day. Style is in harmony with dialect; both products of nature, not artifice.

His translation supports his interpretation. Sappho's verbs are attenuated into nouns, 'terrifies' (*eptoaisen*)[10] becomes the con-ventional love-song term 'a-flutter', 'runs under' (*upadedromēken*) has become 'has stolen' (as in 'has stolen my heart away?'), 'whirrs', like a spinning *rhombos* (*epirrombeisi*) has become 'is humming', pours down (*kakcheetai*), 'covers'; 'hunts' (*agrei*) merely 'seizes'; the violent 'greener than grass' (*chlōrotera poias*) merely 'paler'. Missing also is a sense of the military terminology in the opening stanza: the Homeric 'equal to the gods' has become somehow 'fortunate'. 'Sits opposite' only represents part of the meaning of *enantios*, 'in opposition', as in battle. In the last stanza, the reassurance 'all can be

---

[9]Page, op. cit. 30. It is interesting to note that early critics of *Wuthering Heights*, which was first published under the pseudonym Ellis Bell, found the novel 'forceful'. When it was revealed that the author was in fact Miss Emily Brontë, critics were quick to discover that both characterisation and description in the novel had been adversely affected by the necessary experiential limitations of a woman's life: see Carol Ohmann, 'Emily Brontë in the hands of male critics,' paper read at MLA Women's Forum, December 1970. On the other hand, the author of *Jane Eyre* (Charlotte Brontë) was believed to have experienced the passion portrayed in her book; rumours circulated about her relation-ship with Thackeray. See E. Moers, *Literary Women* (New York 1977) 221-3.

[10]On the meaning of *ptoeō* see H. Frisk, *Griechisches etymologishes Wörterbuch* (Hei-delberg 1960) II.615. The secondary definition 'flutter' given in *LSJ* does not represent the root meaning of the verb, which is cognate to *ptēssō* and *ptōssō* 'crouch in fear' (not to *petomai* 'fly'). In *Od.*22.298-9 *ptoeō* is used to describe the suitors' reaction to Athene holding her aegis above them from the rafters: 'Their hearts were terrified (*phrenes cptoiēthen*); they fled in panic (*ephebonto*) along the hall like a herd of cattle.'

endured' (*tolmaton*) has become a frustrated 'all *must* be endured'.

George Devereux, the anthropologist, sees the poem rather as an emotional outpouring of 'envy' of 'that man', as opposed to simple 'jealousy':[11]

> The core of the problem can best be stated in somewhat colloquial terms: 'What does this man – and indeed any man – have that Sappho does *not* have?' What can a man offer to a girl that Sappho cannot offer? The answer, I think, is obvious (*Od.* 11.249ff.) [this is the passage where Poseidon says to Tyro: 'Rejoice lady, in my love, and as the year goes by you shall bear glorious children, etc.'] and leads to a clinically highly documentable and crucial finding: few women are as obsessed with a (neurotic) feeling of incompleteness – with the clinically commonplace 'female castration complex' – as the masculine lesbian. Moreover, the latter experiences her 'defect' with violent and crushing intensity particularly when her girl-friend is taken away from her not by another lesbian, but by a *man*, who has what she does not have and which she would give her life to have.

According to Devereux, Sappho in the poem is describing the sort of anxiety attack that Devereux has frequently witnessed in homosexual patients.

If Sappho's poem had just been dug out of the sand and if we had never heard of Wilamowitz or looked in Page or read Devereux's article, our interpretation of the poem might be very different. Perhaps it is impossible for any of us to approach Sappho with the same objectivity that we can maintain in reading Emily Dickinson, because we always seem to come to ancient texts with dictionary in hand. But to look at the text itself, without any preconceptions about the identity of the narrator, the poem says: 'That man seems to me like the gods (*isos theoisin*, a designation that in Homer connotes unusual strength) who sits opposite (or in opposition), who hears you (female) speaking sweetly and laughing passionately.[12] This (i.e. hearing you) terrifies my heart in my breast (i.e. the effect of you on me, the narrator, is very different from your effect on 'that man'). For whenever I look at you then I can speak nothing still, but in silence my tongue is broken (*eage*, a verb used to describe broken bones), and immediately a light fire runs under my skin, and with my eyes I see nothing, and my ears whirr, and a cold sweat holds me down, and a shuddering hunts all of me, and I am greener than grass, and from dying little lacking I seem to myself to be (repetition 'to myself' signifies a conclusion, and reference to the narrator, a tran-

[11]George Devereux, 'The nature of Sappho's seizure in fr. 31 LP as evidence of her inversion,' *CQ* n.s. 20 (1970) 22.

[12]On the meaning of *isos theoisin*, see Garry Wills, 'Sappho 31 and Catullus 51,' *GRBS* 8 (1967) 174–83, and M. Marcovich, 'Sappho fr. 31: anxiety attack or love declaration,' *CQ* n.s. 32 (1972) 26.

sition to a new subject).[13] But all is endurable, since even a poor man . . .' – does the poem go on to say that God makes even a poor man rich (as in the introduction to the *Works and Days*), i.e. that there is some hope for change, or eventual triumph?[14]

Looking at the text, it seems fair to say that quantitatively at least the main emphasis in the poem falls on the narrator's feelings. Cf. Moers (n.9) 225 on love-poems by nineteenth-century women: 'They mostly write about Me.' It is important to remember that what she is describing is an illusion, 'he seems to me' (*phainetai moi*), 'I seem to myself' (*phainom' em' autai*). The time is indefinite, the illusion happens over and over: 'whenever I look at you' (*ōs* with subjunctive *idō*). The man has no specific identity; he is 'whoever (*ottis*) sits opposite'. The exaggerated terms in which the narrator's reactions are described add to the sense of illusion: the broken tongue, the sweat that grasps, the shuddering that hunts, and being greener than grass do not portray the condition of the narrator in real life. The phrase 'greener than grass' at the end of the list of symptoms has particular impact. It translates the Homeric 'green fear' for one's life in battle into the context of daily existence. In the same way, the man like the gods in the first stanza is not a Homeric hero but someone sitting opposite a girl. It is as if Sappho were saying that what happens in a woman's life also partakes of the significance of the man's world of war. When she writes a long narrative poem about Hector and Andromache it is to describe their wedding.[15] When she speaks in her poem to 'Aphrodite on intricate throne, immortal' of pursuing and fleeing, it is describing not the grim chase of Hector by Achilles, 'as in a dream one cannot pursue someone who flees' (*Il.*22.200), but the conquest of an un-willing lover, 'if she flees now, soon she'll pursue you.'[16] Her victory is achieved by the intervention of Aphrodite, not through her own powers. In *phainetai moi* also, any change that is to come about must take place through endurance. As a woman, she must rely on the special weapons of the oppressed, miracles and patience.

This interpretation may not tell us everything we want to know about the poem, but I think at least it reveals what the poem is *not* about. There is nothing specifically stated in the poem about jealousy of a rival. What the man has that she (the narrator) doesn't have (*malgré* Devereux) is not male generative capacity but physical

---

[13]On *eage* as 'is crippled', see M. L. West, 'Burning Sappho,' *Maia* 22 (1970) 311, and Marcovich, op. cit. (*supra* n.12) 27-9. On the structure of the poem, see Helmut Saake, *Sappho-Studien* (Munich 1972) 53-4.

[14]On the contents and translation of the fifth stanza, see West, op. cit. 312-13.

[15]This point was suggested to me by Dr Marilyn Skinner.

[16]On Homeric vocabulary in Sappho's poetry, see esp. Irena Kazik-Zawadzka, *De Sapphicae Alcaicaeque elocutionis colore epico* (Wroclaw 1958).

strength: he seems 'like the gods' while she is faint and powerless.[17] What she (the narrator) feels is not jealousy but the response of lovers to beauty in their beloved: when the suitors see Penelope in *Odyssey* 18 'their knees were loosened, and their hearts were beguiled with passion' (212). As for Sappho's style, if being untraditional is artless, then we can agree (in Page's words) that she is 'without artifice'. But it might be fairer to comment on the dramatic personification 'trembling hunts me down' or her conversion of Homeric formulae, e.g. taking 'like the gods' from the context of war to the struggles of emotion, and turning the conventional 'green fear' into the startling, entertaining 'greener than grass am I'.[18] The sense of illusion that she creates in the opening 'he seems' and its echo 'I seem to myself' in the fourth stanza is one of the first expressions of what will later become one of the primary concerns of poetry and philosophy: the effects of the imagination.[19] The deliberate generality of the poem, the absence of proper names and specific references to time and place, indicate that this poem is meant to bring to mind no particular place or occasion. It tells of 'that man – whoever' and of the narrator's reactions 'whenever I look at you'.[20] It is no more directly representative of the historical Sappho's feeling at any given moment in history than the sonnet 'Th' expense of spirit' is a transcript of a day in the life of William Shakespeare.[21]

To recapitulate: biographical criticism, in the case of the women poets Dickinson and Sappho, may keep us from seeing what the poets say. Dickinson's dignified, remote poem about disappointment becomes an outcry of sexual frustration; Sappho's song about the weakness of a woman in love a jealous admission of penis envy. Applying assumptions our society makes about 'normal' female psychology to the work of women poets can do little to advance our understanding of their poems. This is not to say that their poems are not different because they are by women; I think perhaps they are. Dickinson writes about her 'inner life' and Sappho about her love for

[17]On the contrast implied between mortal and immortal, see McEvilley, op. cit. 171, and G. Aurelio Privitera, 'Ambiguità antitesi analogia nel fr. 31 LP di Saffo,' *QUCC* 8 (1969) 37-80.

[18]On Sappho's use of Homeric vocabulary and unusual metaphor, see Marcovich, op. cit. 26–32.

[19]On imagination and reality in this poem, see also McEvilley, op. cit. 171, and on the connotations of *phainesthai*, Helmut Saake, *Zur Kunst Sapphos* (Munich 1971) 20.

[20]But cf. for example C. M. Bowra's appealing recreation of the circumstances from his own imagination; *Greek Lyric Poetry*[2] (Oxford 1961) 184-7. Wilamowitz, of course, read *Agalli*, which helped to particularise the occasion.

[21]Douglas L. Peterson, 'A probable source for Shakespeare's Sonnet CXXXIX,' *Shakespeare Quarterly* 5 (1954) 381-4, shows that 'Th' expense of spirit' is based on a handbook description of the consequences of lust.

her female friends and the pleasures of singing and being together because these activities, not war or games or government, were the experiences that her society and times permitted to women. Those who are secluded in some way from the concerns of the larger society are by necessity thrown on to themselves and thus have time and scope to express what others, in more diffracted contexts, do not have time to articulate or to understand. Such enforced withdrawal has made women's poetry distinctive and influential.

10

Advice on How to
Read Sappho

Few serious students of English literature would begin to study the
works of Jane Austen or of Emily Dickinson by first looking in a
commentary. But students of Sappho must inevitably approach her
poetry through the medium of scholarship; their initial contact with
the poetess thus comes through another's eyes, with all the advantages of the scholar's range of knowledge, and with all the
limitations imposed on him by his culture.

Saake's book[1] in its first chapter acknowledges the pervasive
importance of this interpretative medium, and sets forth concisely in
historical perspective the premises on which each scholarly interpretation has been based. We can learn quickly from his survey
which fragments different scholars had before them, and the principal focus of their interpretations. This accurate listing of who has
done what, in itself a valuable service, also reveals in microcosm
painful general truths about classical scholarship – we ride against
each other, as if in ritual combat, so absorbed in battle that we ignore
works of criticism outside our field, and seem oblivious of potential
allies within it. Work is repeated that has been capably done before;
new approaches are not seriously considered.

Saake concludes his survey by describing what he finds to be the
concerns of present Sapphic scholarship: the problem of the ordering
of her books of poetry, methods of interpretation, and the dating of
her life. In the next chapter he addresses himself directly to the
evidence for and research on the chronology of her biography, with
its important ramifications for the question of whether she in-
fluenced Alcaeus. In a discussion that carefully distinguishes between established historical information (such as the dates of
Myrsilus and Pittacus) and sensible guesswork (Sappho would have

[1]Helmut Saake, *Sapphostudien. Forschungsgeschichtliche, biographische und liter-
arästhetische Untersuchungen.* München, Paderborn, Wien: Verlag Ferdinand
Schöningh, 1972.

been twenty at the time of her exile), he accepts Suidas' birth date of 612, which makes Sappho contemporary with Alcaeus, and thus renders the question of her influence or supposed archaism irrelevant. Saake then illustrates the direction he believes critical interpretation of Sappho's poems should take, by commenting on the structure of her major poems, and by demonstrating the conscious and innovative artistry involved in their creation, summarising recent research, and adding many helpful observations of his own, especially on sound patterns and thematic repetition. He indicates at frequent intervals how Page's characterisation of Sappho's style as naïve and artless is without foundation in the text of the poems themselves. One only wishes that Saake had stated in more detail his views on Sappho's use of Homeric language (see now M. Marcovich in *CQ* n.s. 32 [1972] 19-32), and on the insights that can be derived from psychology and linguistics.

The book has useful indices of ancient and modern authors and a comprehensive bibliography up to 1971, which should include also Garry Wills' 'Sappho 31 and Catullus 51,' *GRBS* 8 (1967) 174-83 and G. Aurelio Privitera's 'Ambiguità antitesi analogia nel fr. 31 LP di Saffo,' *QUCC* 8 (1969) 37-80. In *Sappho-Studien*, together with *Zur Kunst Sapphos: Motiv-analytische und kompositionstechnische Interpretationen* (Munich 1971), his preliminary discussion of interpretation of the texts and evaluation of her style, Saake has performed a valuable service for all students of Sappho, by distinguishing between what Sappho wrote and what critics have said about her, and by focussing attention once again on Sappho's merits as an artist.

11

Semonides on Women

Twenty years ago classicists did not devote much thought to the long iambic discourse on women attributed to Semonides of Amorgos (seventh century B.C.), which explains how Zeus made women's minds (*noos*) separately from men's and describes how he created destructive types of women from pigs, foxes, dogs, the earth, the sea, asses, ferrets, horses, and monkeys, along with one good type – from bees. Now Lloyd-Jones's excellent new text, translation and commentary provide welcome confirmation that classicists no less than other scholars respond to the social and intellectual climate of their own times.[1]

Lloyd-Jones's edition has the distinct advantage of being accessible also to the Greekless reader while being informative and helpful to the classicist. Quinton's illustrations, though the two dimensions of high-contrast black and white cannot do sculpture justice, remind the reader that the poet meant his hearers to imagine as well as to analyse. A lucid preface sets the poem in historical perspective; notes on individual lines discuss with admirable clarity and conciseness the complex problems of interpretation that inevitably beset ancient texts. One wishes only that the Greek words discussed were accompanied by English translations, for the benefit of all readers. Appendices add welcome perspective: included are the newly discovered fragment of an epode of Archilochus, likewise concerned with women and with sex, and Addison's version of Semonides' poem, in which English ethics replace the Greek poet's emphasis on women's ignorance and laziness (e.g., 'sits by the dungheap' becomes 'her family is not better than a dunghill').

Since so little historical evidence about Semonides' period survives, it is tempting to interpret his poem as literal historical data about the Greek attitude toward women, especially since his characterisation of the lazy, amoral female corresponds closely to the sentiments expressed by his contemporary Hesiod about Pandora

[1] *Females of the Species: Semonides on Women.* Edited, translated and with commentary by Hugh Lloyd-Jones, with sculptures by Marcelle Quinton (London 1975).

and women in general.[2] But Lloyd-Jones sensibly emphasises that one can expect this and other poems in iambic metre to take extreme critical stances and that the views on women expressed in the poem are not necessarily those of the poet in private life, nor are they necessarily shared by the whole of his society. The work was meant to amuse, and should therefore not be taken (any more than should Juvenal's sixth satire) as a record of widely held feelings or observed behaviour. The school texts and Sarah Pomeroy's recent study of women in classical antiquity do not really broach this issue, at once classifying the poem as satirical and regarding it as a statement of misogyny, as if (to use an example from Juvenal himself) Messalina represented a norm, and disapproval of her conduct expresses the poet's misogyny and our consent to it. Additional support for an interpretation of the poem as social satire may be found in Semonides' choice of *animals* for most of his characterisations of women. The beasts whose untamed instincts lead themselves or their societies into danger appear not only in Aesop's ethical fables, but in the violently retributive plots of iambic poetry; for example, Archilochus' poetic adversary is Lycambes the wolf-walker (see G. Nagy in *Arethusa*, 9.2 [1976] 191–205). We are only beginning to understand how much we have misconstrued in ancient poetry by interpreting artifice and art as literal biography and history. Lloyd-Jones reminds us that, for all the negativism of Semonides' and Hesiod's statements, prominent roles assigned to the heroines of Homer and of Greek tragedy indicate that the Greeks also took women seriously as people. By dramatising the issue of women's rights, as, for example, in the *Antigone* and the *Medea*, Lloyd-Jones suggests that the Greeks at least raised questions that no previous society thought worthy of consideration.

But it is easier to admire the zeal with which Lloyd-Jones draws assurance from Greek intellectual debate than to accept his implication that *writing* about women's role indicates a serious political interest in women's 'liberation' or in reform of their traditional status. The inherited myths from which the epic bards and the dramatists drew their plots reiterate that women's proper place is in the service of their husbands or nearest male relative. Heroines merit support and attention only in the process of searching or waiting for their allotted men: even the admirable Penelope disappears from view as soon as Odysseus returns and claims her.[3] While she waits

[2]On the dangers of deducing generalities from particulars, see esp. David Hackett Fischer, *Historian's Fallacies* (New York 1970) 109-10; on Hesiod's attitude toward women, see Marylin Arthur, 'Origins of the Western attitude toward women,' *Arethusa* 6 (1973) 24-5.

[3]On the tendency of women in the myths to disappear after marriage, see above, pp.42-4.

for Odysseus, she employs only those skills appropriate to a woman: weaving, deceiving, indecision. The courage and mind (*noos*) that can effect return from death and ultimate triumph are reserved for her husband, Odysseus. The women in dramas who take initiative, Clytemnestra, Medea, even Antigone, end badly regardless of their motives. The plots of tragedies so often concern the fortunes of females because women were considered powerless by nature, and tragedy is the genre that celebrates man's inability to triumph over forces beyond his control. Choruses are frequently composed of women because by convention a chorus can never act to prevent the disasters it must witness.[4]

Semonides' poem, though with the extreme imagery and mechanical exaggeration that we generally associate with satire, expresses the same basic evaluation of female nature. Women's actions, as the opening line states ('Zeus made women's minds separately'), display an absence of the male type of *noos*, which provides the ability to discriminate between good and evil, life and death. For example, the vixen woman calls 'a good thing bad and a bad thing good; her attitude is never the same' (lines 10-11); the earth woman 'knows nothing, bad or good' (lines 22-3), including not enough to come in out of the cold; the sea woman 'has two characters' (*duo noei*, literally, 'thinks two things', line 27); the dog woman responds neither to threats nor to persuasion; the ferret woman steals and sacrilegiously eats offerings left for the gods; the amoral monkey woman 'does not mind being laughed at' (line 79). In addition, the bad women are destructively self-indulgent, stuffing themselves (not their families) with food, eager for sex, ignoring their housework. The bee woman, by contrast, is defined not by what she does for herself but by what she does for her husband: she is specifically praised (as is Penelope) for being different from others of her sex.

For the Greeks, from the eighth century on well into the Hellenistic period, feminine virtue could be most easily defined in terms of obedience and chastity, that is, conformity to *male* norms for female behaviour. Meanwhile the female artist Quinton conveys the basic meaning *for women* of Semonides' poem more eloquently than her male scholar collaborator: the animal women all have dynamic, distinctive expressions, but the bee woman has wings, a long back, and no face.

[4]On the appropriateness of women for choruses, see above, ch.1, n.14.

12

Vellacott on Women

Philip Vellacott in his essay 'Women in Tragedy'[1] starts by asking us to forget contemporary sensitivities to women's roles. One sympathises, since current approval for women who act decisively can encourage us to think that Medea and Hecabe are better off somehow than Deianeira, simply because Medea and Hecabe did what they set out to do.[2] But while Mr Vellacott warns us about feminist criticism, he never says anything explicit about the premises of his own approach to tragedy. So one is left wondering whether his assumptions about Greek dramatists and audiences are any more soundly based than the feminists' or less distorted by current critical fashions.

Were the Greek dramatists basically ironists, working at once both for and against their audience, undercutting the social norms presented in inherited myth? Vellacott's notion of the ironic dramatist appeals because it assures modern readers that the dramatist himself shared some of their negative responses to Greek values; we are flattered to think that we who see these ironies are in fact cleverer than the original audiences. That both Aeschylus and Euripides died in exile appears to support the notion that their views were unacceptable to their public, that 'popularity must have been one of the bitterest trials Aeschylus or Euripides had to bear'. But recent studies have shown that such stories of poets' isolation and exile are fictitious, commonplaces of literary biography.[3] No reliable evidence in fact exists to show how audiences reacted to specific incidents in these or any other dramas. What we do know is that the Athenians voted to give Aeschylus and Euripides choruses throughout their lifetimes, and that they not infrequently took first prizes. In other words the only historical information we possess shows that the Athenians constantly and repeatedly wanted to hear their plays.

[1] Philip Vellacott, *Woman and Man in Ancient Greece: the evidence from tragic drama*, Carleton Miscellany 18 (1980) 7-70. ·

[2] Cf. above, p.5.

[3] See esp. J. A. Fairweather, *Ancient Society* 5 (1974) 231-75; M. R. Lefkowitz, *CR* 28 (1978) 1-11.

Much better sense to start from the assumption that the dramatists were *not* at odds with their audiences. There is no reason to think that Aeschylus was being *ironic* when he has Clytemnestra make a good case for herself: if she were merely an unfaithful wife, with no other causes to wish to kill her husband, the drama would be less instructive, and certainly less interesting. Iphigenia's death is the first cruel result of a system of divine justice whose workings the chorus of the *Agamemnon* gropes to understand. But her death is demanded by the gods, while Clytemnestra sought no oracle's sanction for Agamemnon's murder. Orestes, by contrast, follows Apollo's orders when he kills his mother and then goes to Athens to stand trial. That Athena casts the deciding vote in favour of Orestes emphasises the god's role in defining justice. Similarly in the last play of the trilogy begun by the *Suppliants*, Aphrodite speaks in support of the one Danaid who did not kill her husband. Both trilogies affirm that the way to get recognition for suffering and wrong is not to commit unsanctioned acts of violence, but to seek and to follow the guidance of the gods.

Not that Aeschylus ever represents that it is easy to determine what is right or to recognise that one is doing it: the Athenian jurors cast equal votes for and against Orestes. In getting the Furies to work for man rather than against Orestes, Athena does not use force but offers them new honours and a vision of the powers they will have in the future. In accepting, the Furies provide an example of the benefits of rule by understanding and consent. But by ending the play with a torchlight procession rather than in full daylight, Aeschylus reminds his audience that the dark power that produced the Furies continues to exist.

Sophocles and Euripides were not necessarily being ironists either, when they let their female characters utter strong complaints about their lot: no complacent and accepting woman could bring herself to kill her own children. Euripides brilliantly makes Medea endow her personal troubles with general significance; she tells the chorus and Creon that clever people and foreigners and women are envied and hated so she can more easily win their sympathy. Sophocles, in a fragment preserved from the lost *Tereus*, has Procne complain about the violent change from girlhood to the loneliness of marriage.[4] Though Vellacott does not mention him, Sophocles clearly recognises the difficulties caused by the traditional definitions of sex roles: in the *Antigone* Creon becomes more angry because the disobedient Antigone is female. Because he must insist on his honour and authority and as a male, he rejects a solution that

[4] Fr. 583 Radt (for translation, see p.20).

would give priority to the female values of caring and acceptance.

The mythology of Dionysus in particular deals with human ignorance and the disasters caused by human anger and impetuosity. Tragedy, in celebrating the power of this deceptively appealing god, represents on the stage stories of dangerously delayed recognition of reality. In portraying women as victims of the traditional values of society, the dramatists asked their audiences to question the consequences of their own daily actions, to see in Medea's frustrations the extreme example of a world that values production of male offspring more highly than gratitude or kindness, and that permits women only the alternatives of violent rebellion or acceptance. Dramas like the *Oresteia* or the *Trojan Women* argue that acceptance of injustice is the less destructive of the possibilities: Hecabe, Andromache and women like them represent the best potential of humankind in Dionysus' world.

Perhaps Mr Vellacott has forgotten that in questioning what human beings think and do the Greek dramatists were carrying out their religious duty. Unlike the Judeo-Christian system, with its fixed written code, the proper worship of Greek gods expects inquiry, the questioning of oracles and prophets, the presentation of opposing points of view. If the question of women's position in society is vividly represented in fifth-century drama, we should not be surprised.[5] The dramatists were not being ironic; they were fulfilling their role as public poets by articulating their audience's interest in society's continuing concerns. That their works portray the problems rather than the solutions is inherent in the nature of drama and the god whose cult it serves.

[5]H. Lloyd-Jones, *Females of the Species* (London 1974) 28; above, p.72.

13

Freud on Women

In 1900 Freud's *Interpretation of Dreams* restored significance to experiences that had long been regarded as transient. His theories of analysis, refined into an orthodox methodology, remain a tool of mental therapy. If these same techniques can also be used to explain the meaning of dreams in the ancient world, we should gain in our understanding of ancient peoples' cultures. Devereux's subject matter intrigues; his credentials (both anthropological and psychoanalytic training, plus study of the Classics) would seem ideal. But brief reflection warns that his undertaking, for all its erudition, cannot easily succeed.[1]

The principal difficulty is that Freud's techniques were designed for live patients, who might further be interrogated or even in turn interrogate the analyst, and whose answers might be checked by interviews with family and friends. But dreamers in Greek tragedies cannot be exhumed for necessary dialogue with the analyst, especially since they are fictional to begin with, like the subjects of this book, Atossa, Io, Menelaus, the Erinyes, Clytemnestra, Rhesus' Charioteer, Hecabe, Iphigenia, and the Danaids. More important still, one cannot question their creators, Aeschylus, Sophocles, Euripides, and whoever wrote the *Rhesus*, about even their *overt* intentions; for example, whether they simply composed these dreams for dramatic effect.

To compensate for the unresponsiveness of these fictional 'patients', Devereux is forced to 'actualise' them, so that the format of psychoanalytic practice may be reproduced. In order to show that Atossa in her dream about Xerxes' yoking the two women to a chariot (*Pers.* 181-96) directly involves herself as participant, Devereux reconstructs her family history from references in Herodotus, specifically concentrating on her bigamous and incestuous marriages and her *probable* reactions to them. Similarly, in order to explain the significance of Clytemnestra's dream in *Cho.* 527-35 about nursing a snake, Devereux takes great pains to show

[1]George Devereux, *Dreams in Greek Tragedy: an Ethno-Psycho-Analytic Study* (Oxford 1976).

that the dream expresses her guilt for never having nursed her son. From this finding and the otherwise undocumented 'fact' that she had never suckled any of her babies (including, along with her four children by Agamemnon, presumably the ill-fated son of Tantalus), Devereux is able to deduce that her breasts were small and firm and hence sexually appealing to Orestes (208).

Regrettably neither Atossa nor Clytemnestra (not to mention Aeschylus) can rise to offer the obvious objections. (a) If bigamy and incest were normal practices in Persia, Atossa might not have had any reason to repress her reactions and thus to dream about them. (b) There is no reason to believe on the basis of Aeschylus' text or evidence in any other ancient author (e.g. Eur. IA 1152 where Tantalus' son is torn from Clytemnestra's breasts) that Clytemnestra didn't nurse at least some of her children (on Devereux' mis-interpretation of the role of Cilissa see B. M. W. Knox's review in TLS 12/10/76 1534). (c) The size of her breasts is not described in the drama, nor would they have been readily visible to the theatre audience (if indeed they were represented at all in the male actor's costume).

There is a tendency throughout the book to interpret almost everything in terms of sexual intercourse. Metaphors, whatever their content, are translated by Devereux into a basic meta-language of the unconscious, with clusters of associations so inflexibly set and syntax so limited that they would appear to be the work of a dogmatic allegorist, with moralistic aims. For example, Io's frightening night visions in PV 645-54, urging her so submit to Zeus, are interpreted as the proved female eagerness (in spite of her protestations) for the male penetration without which no woman's life can be normal or complete, be Io's desired partner her father or his replacement Zeus. Even if we accept that such desires are uni-versal and their enactment therapeutic, further acquaintance with the drama would suggest that the dream primarily expresses Io's fear of loss of autonomy, a feeling reinforced by the chorus in the third stasimon, and directly reflected in Prometheus' submissive stance vis-à-vis Zeus.

What makes the relentless progress of reductionism the more painful is that Devereux occasionally shows what a more open-minded response to a drama might produce. He observes that Helen in myth and in the Agamemnon can naturally be represented by a doublet because it is impossible for any man at any time to possess the real Helen (127). But this insight is quickly discarded in favour of a more therapeutic explanation in which Menelaus rejects (rather than regretfully loses) sight of Helen. Similarly, Devereux sees the wolf in Hecabe's dream who slaughters the fawn torn from her lap (*Hec.* 90-1) as emblematic of male action in the primal scene. But as he himself suggests, the audience for whom Euripides was writing, and the character Hecabe herself (who 'lives' only within the context of this play) would see the wolf (who traditionally represents in Greek literature the envious enemy) as predictive of Polymestor, who will later appear onstage blinded and crawling on all fours (278). Euripides uses such thematic repetition elsewhere for dramatic effect: for example, *korē* denotes 'eye' with unusual frequency in this play which concerns the fate of women (e.g. 972, 1117, 1170).

It would be possible also to enumerate at tedious length the unnecessary confusion forced upon the texts by the sexualising process of psychoanalytic 'translation'. For example, there is no need to consider in any way extraordinary the use of *female* horses to pull a chariot (p.8, cf. Pind. *Pyth.* 2.8, Parmenides B. 1.1 DK) or the representation of exceptional females as tall (p.9, cf. Hom. *Od.*6.107-98, Hdt. 1.60.4). Nor is there any reason why in *Ag.* 426 *keleuthoi* ('paths') should mean seductive 'gait' (p.36). In imposing his own interests and preoccupations the analyst subjects the text that here serves as his patient to the destructive consequences of counter-transference, seducing it to extraordinary co-operation with his wishes, stripping it of its cultural characteristics, forcing it through comparison with other patients (such as the Native Americans he studied earlier in his career) into an archetypal norm.

Devereux's undertaking would have more validity if he could demonstrate a mutually informing relation between the dreamer's life and his dream. But as classicists also need to remind themselves, drama is not life, but instead an artistic genre with limitations of structure and content. If dramas still continue to move us (a phenomenon which *pace* Devereux p.xxxii does not pass unobserved), it is not because they focus on unconscious frustrations, but rather because they concern themselves with the terrifying conflicts produced by family structure. All dramas, even the non-mythic *Persae*, concern families. This phenomenon suggests that the language of the Greek unconscious was more multivalent and less sexually oriented than the distinctively male animalistic associative patterns described in this book by Devereux.

14

Education for Women in a Man's World

I had considered myself something of an authority on women's education after ten years as a student at the Brearley School in New York, four years as a student at Wellesley, and 19 years on the faculty at Wellesley. But I can look at what we do there more objectively now, because for three months in 1978 I was at the other end of the world – the University of California at Berkeley.

Usually the first thing that strikes you about a place is how it looks and feels. At Berkeley there is the wonderful warm air, the shrubbery so green it looks as if it is made of plastic, the utilitarian architecture, the freaks in Sproul Plaza, where the riots took place a decade before; all sorts of people outside, enjoying themselves; co-ed soccer games under the lights at nine at night. Everyone is relaxed, 'laid back' or 'kicked back', mostly dressed alike, women and men in jeans and shirts.

Compared with this, Wellesley looks as if it belongs in England; it is an Oxbridge college, with its Gothic buildings, its formality in dress, its wretched climate, where winter strips all colour from the landscape. In England the rain, in Massachusetts the cold, drives people indoors, forces them apart, makes them struggle to get wherever they want to go. Because one is inside so much, classroom and public space at Wellesley tends to be distinctive and attractive; offices and classrooms at Berkeley are purely functional.

The same is true of living accommodation. Wellesley tells you who you are, Berkeley doesn't. Wellesley then is fine if you like what it is telling you: you belong to the class of educated people; you must share with them a taste for certain things, like Oriental rugs on the floor and art for art's sake. You don't get to ask why, because it is there. At Berkeley you can be whoever you want to be, which is fine if you are somebody, but rather rough on you if you aren't someone yet, and aren't quite sure where you want to go.

Another big difference is the faculty's attitude towards undergraduate students. At Wellesley, as in England, the faculty is there first of all to teach the students, and secondarily to pursue their own interests. At Berkeley the priorities are not always so clear: classes are bigger, graduate students read undergraduate papers. In a big class, faculty members cannot grade the papers themselves because they would put graduate students out of a job and not give them the training they are entitled to. So undergraduate students at Berkeley are more grateful than they should be for a senior faculty member's attention, more bashful than they should be about saying who they are. When they come in they have a first name, maybe, not a last, as if their background did not matter.

Now in one way that is liberating, because students and teachers can then meet at the same level, as if we were in an intellectual communal bath. But in another way this leveling seems destructive, because it robs people of valuable distinctions, like the distinction in level of knowledge between student and faculty member, because it is only when one recognises one's relative ignorance and inexperience that one begins to question, to understand, and ultimately to grow.

I have deliberately left the biggest difference for last: the relative importance of women. At Wellesley, women come first, and women run the institution. There are plenty of women students at Berkeley but the faculty is composed almost entirely of men. When I was there, the classics department had one woman assistant professor (who was on leave) and me (a temporary). Does it matter? I cannot furnish any statistics. A recent study seems to show that single-sex colleges haven't turned out proportionately more professionals than co-ed schools, and it suggests that if the Seven Sisters had been proportionately more successful in the production of 'successful' women, this may only have happened because they got the best students to begin with.[1]

So I can only tell you how it feels to be where women faculty members are not integrated into the system. Women students at Berkeley tell me they are relieved to have a woman professor. Maybe it is that they can talk to me more easily; they can ask me about my experiences, tell me about theirs, the sort of dialogue that everyone at Wellesley takes for granted. I will admit that it is fun sometimes to be a sex object, and to be taken out for lunch by my (male) colleagues – that never happens at Wellesley, where we all go dutch, and men soon learn never to open a door. But under conditions where one is always treated first as a member of the 'weaker' sex, I am not sure a woman can have an equal voice, and the women students must feel somewhat isolated too, as they keep hearing this message that says their biological

[1]See below, p.93, n.9.

make-up is at odds with their intellectual or professional role.

Perhaps I am only saying in an elaborate way that Berkeley is the real world, the real America; that Wellesley is a strange Utopia that tries to give women opportunity to be, at least for a little while, all the things that society really does not encourage them to be.

You may want to argue that it is wrong to try to escape, that you want to be on the frontiers. Well, having been on a frontier, I can tell you that it is exciting and challenging, but I am ready for it. Best not to go to the frontier unless you know who you are and what you are getting into. You may need first to develop certain capabilities: academic skills, certainly; but also self-assurance, self-esteem and the ability to co-operate, talents you will need to have if you are to get anywhere at all in a man's world.

Let me say a little more about the last – ability to co-operate. I do not imagine may of you have read Tennyson's poem, 'The Princess'. It was widely read at the time when women's education was becoming a hotly debated topic. In Tennyson's poem, there is a beautiful women's academy where women wear special costumes and give elegant speeches in an ideal landscape. But the academy disbands, as the result of internal dissent, jealousy: the women behave 'in the usual fashion' as if they were competing for the favours of men.[2]

In her commencement address at Wellesley in 1973, Kate Millett advised the seniors to 'keep in touch'. One does not know how literally she meant that, but metaphorically it is very good advice, easier to follow at the women's colleges, essential when you get out. There is a women's underground at Berkeley, and through it individuals can gain the encouragement and support they often need.

'Keeping in touch' also means that one has to organise to know how to operate the political machinery that controls virtually every aspect of life. At the first level, it means learning to listen and to ask questions, so you can tell whom you can trust and whom you cannot; it means learning parliamentary techniques so you can know how meetings are run, or how to get your way in a meeting. It is harder to get a grasp of these procedures if you haven't had experience in school or in college in running a meeting, or in working to promote your motions, or to get yourself or a friend elected to office.

Women professors in classics took a while to get organised, because not all of us knew how to work together. Some women had got their way in the past only by traditional female methods, complaining, appealing to men to help them, fighting for recognition in

---

[2]A. M. Wells, *Miss Marks and Miss Woolley* (Boston 1978) 2; on Tennyson's use of classical mythology in the poem, R. Pattison, *Tennyson and Tradition* (Cambridge, Mass. 1979) 97-8.

some individual way. Once we began to work together as a political group, pooling our resources, younger women asking older women for advice, we began to make progress. We elected candidates to the association's board of directors, and through the board enacted reforms of several kinds in the profession.

One of our suggestions brought a dramatic change. Every year at the annual meeting of classicists, professors present papers on their research. Since it is considered an honour to present a paper at these meetings, the competition for a slot in the programme has become keen. Before 1974, the programme committee (usually composed entirely of men) knew the names of all the people who offered to present papers at the meetings. Not many women or younger scholars were ever picked for the programme.

The women's caucus asked the board of directors to require that the papers be offered anonymously, that is, that the authors' names be left off and the papers be judged on their contents only. When that was done, the number of women on the programme rose 100 per cent, and the next year 100 per cent again, so that by last year about 25 per cent of all papers were presented by women, which is proportionately about right for the profession as a whole.

The board of directors has unanimously confirmed that the policy be continued, and has insisted that it be followed for all its publications. Even people (and this included some women) who had been against the change had to admit that there had been 'some evidence' of discrimination.

That change could never have been brought about by isolated complaining; organisation and formal, orderly presentation, as so often in American politics, won the day. But organisation is just a beginning, a change that didn't cost money; other reforms will be harder to achieve. One of the most difficult is the question of women's rate of publication. In classics, according to a survey we made in 1972,[3] married men write significantly more books and articles than unmarried men or unmarried women, and married women, with a few exceptions, write the fewest of all. The exceptions are women married to highly paid executives or professionals, who can afford household help. Or, to put it another way, married women need wives, so they can write as much as married men.

The best jobs in our profession go to the people who write the most, though not necessarily the best, as long as it is relatively good. How can women compete, especially women with family responsibilities? Day-care centres help, maternity leaves, flexible teaching

[3]'Report of the committee on the status of women,' *Proc. Amer. Philological Assoc.* 104.1 (1974) 22-8, 63-4; ibid. 105.1 (1975) 23-31.

schedules. But more important still, we need to question the priorities: should not good teaching count just as much as research? Or maybe even more? To make that point, women (and men who agree with them) are going to have to demonstrate in serious ways how their students turn out better, how their minds are just as good: we have to find ways of determining if these assertions are true and of effectively showing why. One way of doing that is by individual demonstration, like teaching at Berkeley; but really to make progress, all of us are going to have to know about each other and to accumulate statistics, so we can show that ability to get on in a man's world is not accidental or exceptional.[4]

[4]As it has been; see esp. M. Kilson, 'The status of women in higher education,' *Signs* 1.4 (1976) 935–42.

15

On Becoming a Cow

No generation has been more aware than ours of the aesthetics of translation, because no generation has depended on translations more.[1] Withdrawn within ourselves, we seem to cope with existence best in our own language. We all admit that much is lost in the process of transmission, yet the disinclination to learn even the most accessible modern languages persists relentlessly. Isolation screens us also from the past. We discern easily in history only what is not foreign to our experience. So we regard the Classics, as through a set of filters, with the quality of light successively altered by changing languages and customs.

The English language distorts transmission in distinctive ways. Rigid word order diffracts the sonority and emphasis of the original. Elaborate, distended verse like A. S. Way's or Gilbert Murray's reflects the notion that poetry is defined by rhyme and artificial vocabulary. The spare prosaic lines of Henry Thoreau and Edith Hamilton reflect the contemporaneous belief that poetry can be defined solely by means of content.[2] But mechanics of versification and changing critical theories do not account for all distortion in translation. Sometimes misapprehensions persist despite a translator's selective ear or careful scholarship. In these cases our own culture seems to work against us, causing us to establish false equivalences between words and institutions. So to transform is perhaps instinctive: all societies simplify what they absorb from other cultures into a contemporary normality of their own. By imposing our conventions on foreign thought, we refine and restructure what we read into a framework we can understand. The process is uncon-

[1] For a bibliography of recent critical work on translation, see Francis L. Utley, 'The strategies of translation,' *Journal of Aesthetic Education* 3 (1969) 141-2.

[2] Translation provides a ready index to contemporary poetics; see Reuben A. Brower, 'Seven Agamemnons', in *On Translation (Harvard studies in comp. lit.* 23: Cambridge, Mass. 1959) 173-95. On Thoreau's translation of Pindar, see Brower, 'The Theban eagle in English plumage,' *CP* 43 (1948) 25-30; on Murray's translations of Euripides, see T. S. Eliot, *The Sacred Wood* (London 1950) 73-4.

scious, and takes place whether or not we translate word for word.[3]

Such cultural adaptation seems to have had particular effect on the interpretation of Greek lyric poetry. The language and society of the Archaic age stand remote from our conceptual vocabulary and industrialised existence. The literary remains are fragmentary; historical information is tantalisingly incomplete. Accordingly it is tempting to fill in the gaps with what we know from later antiquity or from our own experience. The resultant misinterpretations occur in recognisable patterns that reveal the character of our language and civilisation, and the consistency with which our culture blocks comprehension of ancient thought.

The 'conventionalising' process has had a telling effect on most English translations of Aeschylus' *Prometheus Bound*. The problem is not misleading substitution of lexical values or reminiscence of a familiar Latin text; the misinterpretation instead stems from contemporary scientific rationalism. We seem unwilling to suspend our disbelief far enough to believe in metamorphosis.

After Io leaves the stage, beset by another attack of madness, driven by the gadfly, the chorus sings an ode concerning marriage. In a pair of carefully rhymed and balanced strophes they compare marriage beyond one's social station to union with Zeus, which has had such a devastating effect on Io. The ode concludes (901-6) with an epode in excited, syncopated metre, where rushes of short syllables explode the basic trochaic pattern:

> ἐμοὶ δ' ὅτε μὲν ὁμαλὸς ὁ γάμος,
> ἄφοβος ἔφυ· δέδια δὲ μὴ
>   κρεισσόνων θεῶν ἔρωι
>   μ' ἄφυκτον ὄμμα προσδράκοι·
> ἀπόλεμος ὅδε γ' ὁ πόλεμος, ἄπορα πόριμος, οὐδ'
>   ἔχω τίς ἂν γενοίμαν·
>   τὰν Διὸς γὰρ οὐχ ὁρῶ
>   μῆτιν ὅπαι φύγοιμ' ἄν.

'May my marriage be on an equal level – without fear. The marriage I dread is that passion, the inescapable eye of the stronger [gods] may look at me. This is a war that cannot be fought; it is a source of resourcelessness. I do not know who I should become. For I do not see how I would escape Zeus' will.'

[3]The process of cultural 'conventionalisation' is analysed in F. C. Bartlett, *Remembering* (Cambridge 1932, repr. 1960) 268-75. Utley (n.1) 138-41 describes the related process of simplification involved in making a children's edition of *Sir Gawain and the Green Knight*.

The assonance, alliteration, rhymes, and punning repetition of the Greek resist translation. Yet the general meaning seems all too clear. Union with Zeus has dire consequences for the female. The chorus has just seen Io on the stage, crazed, exhausted from wandering, deformed, physically as well as mentally: 'and straightway my shape and mind were turned through (*diastrophoi/ēsan*) and horned, as you see, rubbed by the gadfly, in maddened leaping . . . ' (673-5).[4] Io's twisted form, mind, and horns are the consequences of a god's passion and inescapable eye. Her deformity is the result of the war that cannot be fought, that is a provider of ways (*porimos*) that are not ways-out (*apora*). Their question follows logically: 'I do not have who I might become.' *Gignomai*, 'am born', is the standard term for what was later called *metamorphosis* or *transformatio*, a change of shape.[5] Who will the chorus become? A horned girl? A cow? Marriage even to a mortal, with its usual consequence of pregnancy, inevitably involves physical transformation.[6]

In today's world where god, if god is seen to exist at all, is conceived of in spiritual or philosophical terms, the ancient notion of embodied, present deities seems increasingly difficult to grasp. Perhaps this remoteness from the world of myth explains why the chorus' agonised question 'Who should I become?' has usually been translated into the familiar idiom 'What will become of me?' Smyth's Loeb (1930) has 'and I know not what would be my fate'; Thomson (1932), 'what the end might be I know not'; Hamilton (1937), 'for what could I do'; Grene (1942), 'I would not know what I could do'; Anderson (1963), 'nor can I tell what would become of me'. Only one English translator conveys the fearful meaning of the Greek, and that is Gilbert Murray (1931): 'I know not how I

[4] The usual translation of *chriō*, 'sting', here and at 567 mitigates the ambivalent sensuality of the word's elemental meaning, 'rub' (e.g., *christon*, 480, of prepared drugs). The idea that Io's tormentor may bring her the pleasure that she is trying so hard to avoid is suggested in the suspenseful word order of 567: *chriei tis au me tan talainan oistros*, 'rubs – who? – again – me – who suffers – a gadfly?'

[5] *Gignomai* refers specifically to physical transformation in *Od.*4.456-8 (Proteus into a lion, etc.), Eur. *Bacch.* 1330 (Cadmus into a snake), Ar. *Ran.* 495 (Xanthias into Heracles), and cf. also *John* 1.14 (the *logos* into flesh); *LSJ* lists no separate category for this usage. *Metamorphoō* refers to spiritual transformation in *Rom.* 12.2. On Latin terminology, see W. S. Anderson, 'Multiple change in the *Metamorphoses*', *TAPA* 94 (1963) 1-27. In Sophocles' *Inachus* the specific ἐκβουτυποῦται describes the process (fr. 269 a. 37).

[6] On metamorphosis as renunciation of self, see George Devereux, 'Greek pseudo-homosexuality', *SO* 42 (1968) 87, n.3. Io has been transformed into what her tormentors want her to be, a role she herself hates, and thus tries to destroy (582-4, 747-51). Schizophrenics similarly hate and punish their false conforming personalities; see Ronald Laing, *The Divided Self* (London 1965), pp.100-1.

should be changed.'[7] In his preface, Murray, writing during the years when women in England achieved complete political equality, calls attention to Io as a paradigm of female suffering. His clear literal rendering of this line stands in contrast to the formal King Jamesian diction of the rest of the passage, where words like 'enthroned on high', 'unassuaged', 'all-piercing' are added to even out his heavy rhymed pentameter lines. Current events and an inherited sense of theatrical effect may have helped the great Hellenist to see through the haze of contemporary diction and religious training. The fact that such insight is possible indicates that with awareness and effort other cultural misinterpretations could be prevented.

Specific instances of persistent mistranslation are perhaps rare.[8] But conventionalisation affects interpretation at every level. Perhaps soon a growing awareness of the informing powers of the mind will make the idea of metamorphosis real again, and the true impact of Io's physical deformation and wandering will again be felt.[9] Archaeology, linguistics, and imagination can provide only partial insight into antiquity. Accurate perception must begin with the old adage gnōthi seauton.

[7]The passage seems to be mistranslated in other European languages: e.g., Mazon in the Budé (1931), 'je ne vois point de quelle adresse je pourrais bien user'; Wolde (1938), 'wüsste nicht, wie ich's ertrüge'; Brieva Savatieria (1939), 'No sé qué sería de mi'; Bogner (1949), 'was sollte da werden aus mir'.

[8]The mistranslations of Pyth.3.1-3 and Ol.7.1-3 described by Young (n.7), p.28-30, 69-72, seem ultimately to stem from the imposition of Latin idiom. Jebb's translation of zatheos ('holy') in Bacch.5.10 as 'lovely' and at 2.7 'beautiful' may show the power of positive Victorian thinking at work; similarly at 5.116 eribruchas, 'roaring', becomes 'squealing'.

[9]On the meaning of metamorphosis in human behaviour, see Georges Devereux, 'La renonciation à l'identité: defense contre l'anéantissement', Revue française de psychanalyse I (1967) 101-42.

16

On Becoming a Tree

At Wellesley the Professor of Greek regards herself as the Recorder of Institutional Eccentricity. My predecessor, Barbara McCarthy, wrote the chapter on ritual for our Centennial History.[1] There she describes the significance of our Tree Day in the College's first half-century: in 1916, two years after College Hall burned down, the Tree Day pageant celebrated the triumph of Women's Education, personified by the Vision of the College Beautiful in the person of the Tree Day Mistress.[2] From this once grand Ceremony only the Tree Planting survives – and my Tree Day Lecture.[3] But at least the ability to make fun of something implies appreciation of its value.

Certain features of the Tree Day Ceremony resembled standard fertility rites. There was a Bridal Procession by the Tree Day Mistress and Her Court. Only the Initiated (at least in the old days) were admitted:

> It is the day when none but the members of the College are present, when the gates are closed to the curious to the outside world. It is celebrated about the first week in June, when trees and lawns, in the first freshness of their summer beauty, form a harmonious setting for the quaint and picturesque costumes, as the classes move in stately procession or rhythmic dance across the campus.[4]

But note that this ritual denies a role to men: the Tree Day Mistress came with bridesmaids but without a groom. A procession of classes marked the survival of the institution without direct recourse to normal means of reproduction; the planting of the class tree recalled the myth of Daphne, who by refusing Apollo's advances, managed to survive at least as a representation of herself, a laurel tree, fixed in one place, with her own name (*daphne* means laurel). Surely her fate is to be preferred to Io's, who got involved with Zeus and wound up

[1] *Wellesley College 1875-1975*, ed. J. Glasscock (Wellesley 1975) 235-64.
[2] Ibid. 239.
[3] Ibid. 237.
[4] M. B. Hill and H. G. Eager, *Wellesley the College Beautiful* (Boston 1895) 36. On sacred trees in antiquity, see A. Henrichs, '"Thou shalt not kill a tree": Greek, Manichean and Indian Tales,' *Bull. Amer. Soc. of Papyrologists* 16.1-2 (1979) 85-108.

as a wandering pregnant cow.[5] 'The Song of the First Tree Day' by
Mary Russell Bartlett (1879) testifies that the first Wellesley students
saw in their class tree (a rare evergreen with gold-tipped branches)
unchanging representation of their own youth:[6]

> O fair golden evergreen, shine more and more
> Till the radiant gold doth cover thee o'er
> Till our lives' hoped-for gold in bright showers shall fall
> And the light of our vision envelop us all.
>
> (Chorus)
> O nymph divine
> We're thine, we're thine
> Thy beauty is our chosen shrine
> We'll dare, we'll dare
> Thy fate to share
> Our chosen Nymph
> With golden hair.

The notion of idealised feminine self-sufficiency expressed in
these enthusiastic verses has a certain appeal: the students are striving
to move out of the particularity of everyday life by returning to the
past, with its wood nymphs, and by trying to form a community
with others:

> . . . the gleam of vision ideal shall break
> Through the common and real of our lives for thy sake.

To Jane Ellen Harrison, the first woman historian of Greek religion,
the woman's college (in her case Newnham, Cambridge), with its
celibate existence, offered women the only possibility of individual
life:[7]

> By what miracle I escaped marriage, I do not know . . . Marriage, for a
> woman at least, hampers the two things that made life to me glorious,
> friendship and learning . . . The role of wife and mother is no easy one;
> with my head full of other things I might dismally have failed. On the
> other hand, I have a natural gift for community life. It seems to me sane
> and civilised and economically right. I like to live spaciously, but rather
> plainly, in large halls with great spaces and quiet libraries. I like to wake in
> the morning with the sense of a great silent garden around me . . . If I had
> been rich I should have founded a learned community for women, with
> vows of consecration and a beautiful rule and habit; as it is I am content to
> have lived many years of my life in a college.

---

[5]Above, p.43, 88.
[6]*April Song and Wellesley Memories* (Boston 1912) 88; cf. F. Converse, *The Story of
Wellesley* (Boston 1915) 202 ff.
[7]'Reminiscences of a Student's Life,' (1925) reprinted in *Arion* 4.2 (1965) 345.

The natural environment suggested to these women the best potential of human experience; one catches some of the same idealism in the opening verses of 'America the Beautiful', 'for spacious skies, for amber waves of grain'; certainly our Founder, Mr Durant, took a particular interest in the landscaping of his new college.

Metaphors from nature predominate in songs written by students in Wellesley's first decades: especially the lake, but also the lawns and the trees. I would like to discuss the metaphors in four of these early songs, concluding with our Alma Mater, because I think that they show more clearly even than the Tree Day poem the potential and limitation of the ideal of feminine self-sufficiency.[8] The songs express enthusiasm, affection, cameraderie, but at the same time a sense that what they celebrate is evanescent, ephemeral, offering a shared past rather than a plan for the future.

The 'Crew Song', unlike rowing or football songs in marching time from men's colleges, is set to waltz time; it is in fact a love song, with the lake as the beloved. The narrator(s) of the song depict themselves as going out to meet her, while still managing to keep in touch with the shore: 'but back through the stillness, message of music we send'. In fact as soon as they get out, with no record of what may or may not have happened, they come back to shore again:

> Home again float we in silence, silence unaided by song
> For with each splash of the oar dip
> Memories manifold throng
> Farewell now to the breezes
> And moon of the silvery light
> Beautiful waters of Waban
> Sadly we bid you goodnight.

The lovers' failure is made even more explicit in *Lake Waban*. Here sexual language indicates the lake's dramatic role in the song:

> Lake of Grey at dawning day
> In soft shadows lying
> Waters kissed by morning mist
> Early breezes sighing.

But she is only an illusion:

> Fairy vision that thou art
> Soon thy fleeting charms depart
> Every grace that wins the heart
> Like our youth is flying.

The second stanza speaks of the inevitability of the singer-lovers' departure: 'Happy hours today are ours, Cares are for the morrow.'

[8]Texts from *The Wellesley College Song Book* (Wellesley 1897, 1906).

The third stanza begins active withdrawal: emphasis is now on quality of light, 'gold on thy bosom blowing', and 'memory's gaze'. The 'golden time' remembered will outlast the temporary gifts their beloved Lake has given them in the brief time they were together. The last stanza seems almost mystical:

> Lake of white at holy night
> in the moonlight gleaming.

The lovers are separated, but still joined by a reciprocal concern:

> on the wavelets bear away
> Every care we've known today
> Bring on thy returning way
> Peaceful happy dreaming.

'Step Song' describes still more directly the problems involved in a love affair between a young female and a beloved who is both female and impersonal. In this song, composed for a ritual which marks the progression in time and final departure into the world, the Beloved is the College herself:

> Wellesley our Wellesley, hear our voices in the night
> Wellesley, our Wellesley
> Source of strength and light.

The music once again is waltz time, and the model an actual love song, 'Juanita'. Like Juanita, the beloved remains parted from her lover: 'years shall find us far from thee'; but they will be with each other in their imaginations:

> . . . and we'll ne'er forget thee
> Though we leave thee long.

The situations portrayed in the songs about the Lake and in the 'Step Song' help us understand the remarkable language and sentiments of Wellesley's 'Alma Mater'. The song starts out with the usual expression of affection of the alumnae, foster children, to their foster mother, the Alma Mater. But by the end of the stanza there is a suggestion that she is also their Beloved: she is fickle, 'in every changing mood we love her'. 'Changeful sky, bend blue above her' may of course be a reasonable request for better weather than we usually get in Massachusetts, but the metaphor is suggestive: can the sky (always masculine in Indo-European myth) act as a surrogate for the alumnae in an act of love that these women cannot perform for themselves? In any case the second stanza is unequivocal in its characterisation of the College as Beloved in what is now plainly a courtly love affair:

We'll give our lives and hopes to serve her . . .
a stainless name we will preserve her
Answer to her every call.

As women, of course, they have no choice but to preserve her virginity.

The message these songs convey is at best discouraging: that one must love one's beloved, but must leave her, even though the relationship is aesthetically satisfying, offers sustenance, and engenders respect. Everything after is more sinister,

> . . . other years may bring us tears
> Other days be full of fears.

But the songs offer no suggestions of how to deal with these inevitable difficulties to come. They present the female lovers as well-intentioned, but ultimately ineffectual, except in that they are able to offer loyalty and to promise to continue to serve their beloved.

The mythology of these songs would seem to lend support to the feminists who criticise the women's colleges for having perpetrated stereotypes of female behaviour. Instead perhaps, we should now have marching songs like the men's colleges, with affairs that end in consummation. But one can say of these old Wellesley songs that at least they are realistic in expressing the fears of the future many women felt and feel but are not encouraged to acknowledge. Women's colleges may not have done as much as they should to get females to play a more aggressive role in the world,[9] but at least they have allowed women openly to express some of the problems.

The mythology still has meaning, since its principal ritual survived despite my best efforts. Suppressed in 1970, a planting ceremony was held again in 1971, the year that the Ivy League men's colleges became co-educational. Within a few years, students organised a maypole dance, all female, as at Bryn Mawr. By planting the year tree, we can ensure that this class will survive as an individual like Daphne, as long (of course) as one doesn't get involved with men or leave the campus. Remember Jane Harrison's advice (and it helps to know she spent the last years of her life studying Russian with a girl friend): to survive we must stay together. As Persephone discovered when Hades carried her off to the Underworld, *marriage is death.*

[9]H. S. Oates and S. Williamson, 'Women's colleges and women achievers,' *Signs* 3.4 (1978) 795–806.

Index